TURKEY

SYRIA

LEBANON
Beirut
Damascus

Baghdad

ISRAEL

IRAQ

Port
Said

Amman
Azraq

JORDAN

Suez

Tigris

Nile

Former Hejaz
Railway

Medina

Jeddah • Mecca

JUST–HUGH

Hugh Raymond Leach
REMEMBERED

JUST–HUGH

Hugh Raymond Leach OBE, MBE (MIL)
REMEMBERED

Compiled and Edited by

Susan Maria Farrington
and
Norman J M Cameron

ÆP
Arabian Publishing

Arabian Publishing
50 High Street, Cowes,
Isle of Wight PO31 7RR

First published by Arabian Publishing 2022

Designed and typeset in Baskerville by Nick Avery Design
www.nickaverydesign.co.uk

Maps by Martin Lubikowski FBCart.S., Dip Geog of ML Design
www.facebook.com/MakingMapsWork

Dust Jacket printed by Thomas Leach Colour
Abingdon, OX14 1RL

Printed and bound by Short Run Press Limited,
Exeter EX2 7LW

British Library Cataloguing-in-Publications Data

A CIP record for this title is available from
the British Library

ISBN 978-1-911487-74-6

Every effort has been taken to verify the accuracy of the material in this book
and to gain permission for use of all images.

Desert Night

I have lain below a sea of stars
And gazed into infinity.
While cooling sands held fast the night
The silence touched eternity.

Lines inspired by Hugh Leach, 2016

'In his life, Hugh took on a rich diversity of roles. There was Hugh the soldier, Hugh the diplomat, the circus ring master, the explorer, the writer and scholar, the carpenter and woodworker, the photographer, the cyclist and walker. What united all these different aspects of his character was his deep humanity, his great loyalty to his many friends, his professionalism in everything he did and his 'larkiness', a word that Hugh often used to sum up a sense of fun, adventure, and occasional naughtiness and irreverence.'

Stephan Roman

Foreword

Hugh Leach was a man of parts – parts that in their combination of human and literary achievement on the one hand and extensive exploration in Asia on the other, it may be impossible, in a shrinking world, for anybody again to emulate. The breadth of these parts is comprehensively brought out by Stephan Roman in the opening words of this compilation; little need be added in a Foreword.

However, as a former Chairman of the Royal Society for Asian Affairs, I should like to highlight Hugh's contribution to the Society, not least in his leaving the Society a major bequest. What he meant to the Society was recognised in his lifetime: we created the new post of Historian, not hitherto in the Rules, so that Hugh could serve continuously on Council without the requirement to stand down between periods of service.

Space needs to be found for warm thanks to the team of volunteers who undertook the task of collecting and putting into shape the wide-ranging contents of the compilation. The leader of the team was Susan Maria Farrington, who had also been Hugh's collaborator when he wrote *Strolling About on the Roof of the World*: particular gratitude is owed to her.

Norman Cameron, Sue Farrington's principal assistant in compiling this volume, has pointed out that it does not specifically mention one of Hugh's skills, namely that he was adept in offering votes of thanks. In that spirit I hope that, as we dip into the compilation, we offer a toast to a remarkable man who offered so much to so many.

Sir Harold Walker, KCMG
Past Chairman and Honorary Vice-President
Royal Society for Asian Affairs

شر البلية ما يضحك

Ex Libris Hugh Leach

Preface

*J*ust Hugh is a portrait of Hugh Leach, an end-of-era soldier, diplomat, traveller and, above all, charismatic enthusiast. The title reflects his passion for *Just William* books, one of his many and varied interests. To echo a phrase that Hugh used on the flyleaf of his *Strolling About on the Roof of the World*, the *fons et origo* of these memories was an idea mooted at his memorial service in April 2016, five months after his death.

This book has been written to unite the many affectionate anecdotes and recollections submitted after that service with others previously received for his Royal Society for Asian Affairs (RSAA) obituary, with Hugh's own reminiscences in his later years.

Hugh was first elected to the RSAA in 1962. For over half his long membership, he served as a Member of Council, in 1984 being appointed the Society's first official Historian. He was made an Honorary Vice-President in his final year, 2015. In addition, in 1991 he became an enthusiastic member of the Library Committee (later renamed the Library and Assets Committee), contributing his detailed knowledge of the Society's archives when they were first catalogued. Over the years he gave numerous lectures and presentations to RSAA members, had many articles, reviews or obituaries published in the Society's journal, *Asian Affairs*, and was thus the natural choice to be principal author of the Society's centennial history, *Strolling About on the Roof of the World* (RoutledgeCurzon 2003). An inspiring teacher, Hugh in 1970 gave his first Young People's lecture; in 1992, led the RSAA's first Young Persons' Expedition; and, in 1996, was instrumental in forming the Young Persons' Committee. The culmination was the award of the Society's Lawrence of Arabia Medal in 1998.

After his death in 2015, he left the Society a major bequest, which has secured its immediate future. The following year, the Society established the 'Hugh Leach Memorial Lecture' to be delivered annually on a subject reflecting Hugh's interest in the Middle East and Central Asia.

While the RSAA was a central focus for Hugh, he himself described his life as a 'three ringed circus': the Army, which gave him his first exposure to the Middle

East and many life-long friends; the Diplomatic Service, which cemented his interest in Arabia and its people and culture, followed by a well-travelled and active retirement.

Combining all these elements, and in acknowledging the breadth of Hugh's contribution to the RSAA, members of the Society have brought together these insights into an extraordinary life; by no means a comprehensive biography, but an attempt to put on record the varied and remarkable man he was. He was not alone among the Society's membership in leading an eventful, historically interesting life, but his multi-faceted personality and the wide range of his experiences were of their time and unique.

Proudly holding the RSAA's Lawrence of Arabia medal. The residents of Choumert Square gave Hugh (HRL) a party in celebration of his award.

Acknowledgements

This tribute might be likened to a mosaic: a mosaic of memories from family, friends, colleagues and material gleaned from various published obituaries. Some parts stem directly from recollections and anecdotes from Hugh Leach himself towards the end of his life. For reasons of space and context and to avoid repetition, it has not been possible to include all the contributions in their entirety, but all have been used in some way to reach the finished result.

Hugh's family and executors have agreed to the extensive use of material from his archives, and the editors wish to acknowledge their support in the design and publication of this work.

Those who took part in the collection and editing of the sum of the components were principally Sue Farrington and Norman Cameron, with significant support from John McIlwain, who shared his considerable knowledge of such publications. In turn, they are grateful to the Royal Society for Asian Affairs: Adrian Steger, FRCS, Michael Ryder, CMG, and Briony Watson, together with Marilyn Arnott, Paulette Craxford and Morven Hutchison, MBE; to Major Martin Timmis for guidance on military matters; to Thomas Leach Colour who generously printed the dust jacket in memory of Hugh, a former director of the company; to the design skills of Nick Avery of Nick Avery Design and to the team at Short Run Press for printing and binding the book. Finally, to Peter Harrigan of Arabian Publishing (AP), whose positive response to a suggestion from Stephan Roman now enables *Just Hugh* to join *Seen in the Yemen*, an earlier AP title by Hugh.

Most importantly, thanks are due to all the following who contributed advice, background information or memories of Hugh: Jon Aldridge, Sultana Al-Quaiti MBE, Glenda Anderson, Joy Ashworth, Gary Baiden, Helen Baker, Chris Barltrop, Penny Bassett-Jones, Diana Berridge, Lady Sarah Biffen, Michael Bishop, Alexa Broad, Captain Guy Burn, Martin Burton, Meriel Buxton, Marilyn Cameron, Pixie Campbell MBE, David Challis, Dr Peter Clark OBE, Bill Colegrave, Ian Coomber, Eliza, Lady Conyngham, Paulette Craxford, Professor Werner Daum, Mark Dickerson, John Doble OBE, Colonel Bruce

Duncan MBE, Jeff Eamon, Dr Alexander Evans OBE, Alun Evans CMG, Richard Fell CVO, Robert FitzPatrick, Dr Julius Green, Mark Griffen, Keith Hamilton, Anne Harcombe, John Harding, Jenny Harding-Rolls, John Hare OBE, Chris Hawley, Revd Bob Hicks, Harriet Howard, Anthony (Tony) Howell, Marian and Dave Hurle, Charlie Jacoby, Douglas Johnson, James Johnstone, the Leach family, Alison Lester, The Hon. Ivor Lucas CMG, Lionel Mackay, John Macpherson OBE, John Malcolm, Peter Morris, Trevor Mostyn, Adrian Mutton, Dr Tim Myatt, James Nash MBE, Dr Bijan Omrani, Dr Toby Parker, General Sir Robert Pascoe KCB MBE, Thanos Petouris, Graham Reuby, Stephan Roman CMG, Colonel David Sands, Clara and John Semple, Don Stacey, Adrian Steger FRCS, Neil Stratford, Garry Stuart, Paul Swift, Sir Geoffrey Tantum CMG OBE, Captain Charles Timmis, Jane Tippett, Sir Roger Tomkys KCMG, David and Trisha Tomlinson, Michael Triff, Anna Vaudrey, Thelma and Roy Vernon, Rosalind Wade Haddon, Colonel Tom Walcot, Sir Harold Walker KCMG, Ann Ward, Jane Warne, Sir Gerald Warner KCMG, Sarah Wearne, Peter Wilcox, Ian Williams, Lieutenant Colonel Jeremy Williams OBE, Rebecca Wilmshurst, Steve Wilson and Brigadier C W (Bill) Woodburn, together with members of staff of Abingdon School, Arabian Publishing, Army & Navy Club, Jaguar Land Rover, Natural History Museum, Pitt Rivers Museum, Oxford, the Royal Russell School, Croydon and Taylor & Francis.

Acknowledgements – Illustrations

Abingdon School: pp.7, 90; Arabian Album Chameleon3: p.56; Annette Bosanquet: p.85; Peter Danby-Smith: p.120; Sue Farrington: pp.18-9,24,34,39,73,75-7,80,95 lower right, 97-8,100,104,115,116x2,118; Anthony ffrench Blake OBE: p.113 top left; Harriet Howard: pp.130,131; Marian and Dave Hurle: p.92; Andrew Johnstone: p.21; John McIlwain: p.109; Peter Morris: pp.42 lower, 54 lower left; Royal Russell School, Croydon: dust jacket, p.89; Shutterstock: pp.xiii,5,12,19,26,33,44,47,56,59,69,87, 99,105; Sound Stills: p.135; Adrian Steger: p.86; @garry_stuart: pp.111 lower, 112 centre; Thomas Leach Colour: pp.5,6; Jane Tippett: p.71; Rosalind Wade Haddon: p.102; Rebecca Wilmshurst: p.x,114,142.

The majority of images come from Hugh's personal archives. However, we are not to know how many of these were taken by Hugh, himself a keen photographer, or whether they were sent to him by his family or friends. We apologise, therefore, to anyone whose images may inadvertently not have been credited.

CONTENTS

(continued overleaf)

Al-Shadhili Mosque in Mokha, Yemen

أهلاً وسهلاً *

INTRODUCTION
An Extraordinary Life

Hugh Leach died on 14 November 2015. At his funeral sixteen days later, his nephew, Paul Swift, delivered the eulogy for, as he put it, 'an extraordinary man who led an extraordinary life.

'By any measure [my Uncle Hugh's] contribution to the life of this country and beyond was significant, as witnessed by the prominence of the obituary in the *Daily Telegraph*** where his exploits as a soldier, diplomat, explorer and writer were documented.

'Hugh and his twin sister Shirley, my mother, were born on 5th May 1934 to Phyllis and Victor

Hugh's mother, Phyllis Leach (née Holmes) (1900-1934).

Leach. Sadly, Phyllis died during childbirth. Victor, or VJ as he was known, never remarried and the lives of the twins and their older siblings David and Christine were to be shaped by this tragedy. Shirley spent most of her early childhood living with her maternal grandparents while Hugh grew up in the family home, and it was during these formative years that Hugh made what was by his own reckoning one of the most important attachments of his life, to his sister Chrissie.

'They were a formidable pair, roaming the countryside, catapults at the ready like characters from one of his beloved *Just William* books. At home numerous nannies struggled to cope with them, including one who, according to Hugh, "took one look at us and left without even unpacking her bags".

*An Arabic greeting meaning 'Hello and Welcome'.
**This obituary, dated 26 November, was later to be followed by *The Times* on 18 December 2015.

Opposite: Hugh aged eleven and a half.

'Returning to the fold in the early years of the war, Shirley was initiated into Hugh and Chrissie's gang with a series of "nerve tests", one of which involved her jumping from a first-floor window, resulting in a severely sprained ankle. This didn't deter their lust for reckless adventure. Periodically VJ would receive phone calls at work from neighbours complaining, "Your children are on the roof again Mr Leach", while staff of the Abingdon branch railway would routinely curse those Leach children for their fare-dodging, games of dare and bending pennies beneath the wheels of locomotives.

'At Abingdon School, Hugh's future career began to take shape. For example, one important soldierly skill developed during this time was his prowess with the bugle – indeed it earned him the soubriquet "Lips Leach". Who knows what part this oscular dexterity with the bugle played in his military career. But within the family it provided a suitably solemn send-off for much loved pets and also kept us entertained at Christmas. One year it was a recital made up of the official Foreign Office calls for summoning drinks in diplomatic missions around the world. And, of course, Lips Leach would mark the Act of Remembrance in the church at Hinton St George each November.

'Much of Hugh's career was spent overseas, which meant that direct contact with the family was episodic. Nevertheless, he was a prolific writer of letters and postcards and we were never short of news about his exploits once we had deciphered the hieroglyphics that passed for his handwriting. Any mention of this would prompt the retort, "Well apparently my written Arabic is very readable"!

'While we were all quietly proud of his achievements and the esteem in which he was held in various fields, it was his presence that we valued most. And Hugh was one of those people who had real presence. Wherever he went Hugh made an instant and lasting impression upon people. He was physically striking not just on account of his height – perhaps "bearing" is a better word – but also his face with that strong jawline and open countenance, professorial spectacles and his dress-sense – English gent accessorised with a *pakul* (a tribal hat).

'To my cousins and me, he seemed like a giant. Seeing him so infrequently he grew taller in our imaginations. As a boy I remember pondering how he could possibly fold his six-foot four-inch frame into a tank. My impeccable child logic told me the reason he commanded the tank was because he was the tallest member of the crew and needed to poke his head out of the turret.

'By character, Hugh was a romantic. I don't mean that he was a flowers-and-chocolates type of man, but that he had an idealised view of the world, or

HRL with his twin sister, Shirley.

rather of a world that he wanted to live in. His was a world of adventure and exploration, of trekking, of tramping and – a wonderful Hugh Leach word this – of "vagabonding". His was a world of circuses and steam engines, of classic cars and motorbikes, uniforms and tweeds, books and scholarship, high tea and amber nectar. The homes he made, especially the ones in Choumert Square and at Brettingham Court, were, like the man, unique (although my cousin Fiona recalls visiting the home of one of Hugh's heroes, T. E. Lawrence, and being struck at how like Hugh's it was).

'Hugh revelled in being old-fashioned, often coming across as "other-worldly" or eccentric. While he baulked at so much of the modern world – and modern was a relative term for Hugh when it came to things like cars and cameras – I never heard him express any bitterness or cynicism about younger generations. Indeed, Hugh had an enviable capacity, doubtless a prime asset for a diplomat, for striking a relationship with anyone irrespective of age, class or creed. Everywhere he went, people warmed to him. He seemed to meld effortlessly into the community, including here in Hinton St George.

'Part of our family folklore was Hugh's perennial quest for "Mrs Leach". Down the years many candidates came forward but invariably failed to meet the stringent criteria that Hugh had set for the perfect wife. Endurance tests on foot or bicycle seemed to feature quite prominently as I recall.

'In retirement Shirley and Hugh's many happy walking holidays together invariably involved a lot of hard work for Shirley, not just because of Hugh's failure to make allowances for his little sister but, in her own words, "because I would have to arrange everything while Hugh was busy flirting with all and sundry". Visiting him at Hurst Manor, his nursing home, not long before his death we learned that he was still dispensing proposals of marriage, much to the amusement of the female residents.'

Paul concludes with a quotation from George Borrow's *Lavengro*, a book which Hugh loved: 'There's night and day, brother, both sweet things; sun, moon, and stars, brother, all sweet things; there's likewise a wind on the heath. Life is very sweet, brother; who would wish to die?'

EARLY YEARS

A Family Business

'Your family firm has done so much for the church all over the world'

Extract from a letter received from the office of the Archbishop of Canterbury, 2011

Hugh described himself as coming from a strict Methodist Tory family – 'very middle, middle class'. It was a large one too. Hugh's grandfather had ten or eleven children and Hugh had three siblings, David (1929–2016), Christine (1932–2014) and Shirley, Hugh's twin – and ten nieces and nephews.

The Leaches were very religious: Methodist by background. Hugh's grandfather, Thomas, was a lay preacher and his father, Victor John (1897–1975) also a preacher, was, as well, organist and choirmaster at Trinity Methodist Church in Abingdon for forty–seven years. Ecumenical in his thinking, VJ believed that there should be only one church in the world. His life's work was towards uniting Methodists and the Church of England.

Hugh was a shareholder in the family business, Thomas Leach Colour, which was the oldest progenitorial family firm of printers and publishers to the Church of England. It was founded in Abingdon in 1901 by Hugh's grandfather Thomas as Thomas Leach Ltd. He ran it till he was eighty-nine when Hugh's father succeeded in tandem

HRL's grandfather Thomas Leach who, in 1901, founded the family business Thomas Leach Limited (now named Thomas Leach Colour).

Opposite: The Leach family (from left to right) Shirley, David, Victor John (VJ), Christine, Hugh.

with his uncle, Frederick. Both men died while in harness to be succeeded by Hugh's older brother David.

Hugh was particularly affected by his father's death and its aftermath, both of which were unusual. While sitting on the edge of his bed getting benefit from a therapeutic ray lamp, his father suffered an aortic aneurysm and fell onto the lamp, setting the room on fire. The house was saved but VJ was dead.

Hugh, *en poste* in Cairo, returned for the funeral. On the bedside table, Hugh found the bible his father read every night. 'I was intrigued to see where the blue book-mark was, again a little singed, which presumably he had read the night before he died. I opened the bible and at the most central point of the page... was this verse: "And which of you shall take into the house a lamp and place it on the floor and not on the table." I was so overwhelmed I closed the bible and left the house immediately. I promise you that was a true story.'

Hugh emphasised to friends the deep effect that this experience had on him. Although it is difficult to find an exact replica of the verse, there are texts, closely similar, one of which must have made the impression Hugh described, for example Mark 4.21 or Luke 8.16.

Hugh much enjoyed talking to the staff. His father had run the company as a family, true to his faith claiming that the staff were the most important thing and money unimportant. One lady worked there for fifty-seven years.

Thomas Leach Ltd, Abingdon 1930s.

Abingdon School *c*.1939.

Amongst many other printing services, including the cover of this book, Thomas Leach Colour continues to produce Christmas and Easter cards. Hugh expressed pride that his grandfather had invented the offertory envelope for when a parishioner is unable to go to church. Another incident he recounted with pride was when he was in India and visited St James's church in Delhi: as he was coming out, the priest said 'Nice to see you. The only Leach we know is Thomas Leach!' Any cleric over sixty would know the Thomas Leach company.

An Education in Abingdon

Hugh attended the kindergarten at St Helen and St Katharine school, an Anglo-Catholic school in Abingdon which had eight kindergarten boys aged around four or five. In 1942 he went as a day boy to Harewood House preparatory school, which had been evacuated from Bexhill to Abingdon. The next year, the school went back to Bexhill taking Hugh with them, as a boarder.

At thirteen he took the common entrance exam and won a boarding scholarship to Abingdon School. For his last three or four years there he became a day-boy, when brother David was called up for National Service, as his father always wanted someone living at home. According to Hugh, he and Shirley never fully appreciated the situation of their father: the loss of his wife, his running the business, his four young children.

HRL (left) with two friends at Harewood House prep school.

Graduating from a Box Brownie, Cadet Leach studies his Voigtländer camera.

HRL in his rowing blazer. He was described as folding up his long legs into the cox's seat like a stick insect.

Hugh confessed to being lazy at school. However, he did show promise at English and a master, Don Willis, spotted his potential at an early stage and told him he could become editor of the school magazine, the *Abingdonian*. Hugh was hurt that his father said he was not old enough yet.

Hugh had little talent or appetite for team sports, being something of a loner at that stage and, as always, preferring a good walk. He did have some ability at cross-country running and hurdling but found his sporting niche as a cox at rowing. As a younger boy he had rowed a skiff on the Thames and graduated to be cox of the Abingdon school eight. He also coxed the school's 'four' to a win at the Marlow regatta.

It was at Abingdon that three of Hugh's later passions were nurtured. One was photography, mainly black-and-white. Hugh had a Box Brownie camera at school, graduating, via a Voigtländer, to the classic Leica.

Another passion was for motorbikes. Hugh had his own as a schoolboy, although how this was achieved was something of a mystery, as bikes were not allowed; Hugh was one of a small gang of boys who kept his in a ditch on the edge of a neighbouring airfield.

George Duxbury, the 'Mr Chips' of the school, had a motorbike and was a great influence on Hugh in his schooldays. 'GD' was a 'dear man' who taught Latin. He wore little round glasses and chugged to school each day on a 150cc BSA. Hugh remembered taking off the cylinder head and decoking this machine during a school break one day. Visitors to Abingdon are still shown where Hugh had famously ridden his bike indoors, having smuggled it upstairs after dark one night.

Even if you did not know Hugh well, you would more than likely have become aware of his passion for bugles, a passion nurtured in the CCF force at Abingdon School. From the banks of the Nile to the source of the Oxus, from private lawns in Sussex to the town square in Crewkerne and, of course, on every one of his expeditions, Hugh and his bugle were inseparable. At least eight assorted bugles and trumpets were in his possession at the time of his death.

Bugles and trumpets were to become a lifelong passion.

From a musical family, Hugh was the only one who liked brass band music. He colourfully described in his radio broadcast *A Bugler's Life* (Appendix A) how he acquired his first bugle, joined the school cadet force as a bugler and started a fire at the CCF camp to make sure he got a chance to play it. For the rest of his life the bugle was to be a constant companion.

Major Sam Parker was head of the school cadet force. He had bad war-injuries and did not have the temperament to be a good master but, like Duxbury, was a powerful influence. He had chosen Hugh, as senior cadet of the Abingdon School cadet force, to stand on the Victoria Memorial outside Buckingham Palace for the coronation of the Queen in June 1953.

Hugh thought at first that he would like to be a vet, and took a holiday job with the local vet but, persuaded by Parker, changed his mind and decided on the army instead. Time was against him – as mentioned, Hugh had been lazy and the application had to be in before he reached his nineteenth birthday. However, with extra tuition in Latin from Duxbury, Hugh managed to get in. He used to claim that the only distinction he shared with Sir Winston Churchill was that they had both passed last into Sandhurst. The civil service exam required 360 out of 800 marks, and a pass in maths. Both scraped in on 360.

Duxbury died tragically, and in later life Hugh felt very privileged not only to be invited to give the address at the memorial service in the school chapel but to be allowed to wear the Duxbury Tie – normally for boys who did academically well, which did not, of course, include Hugh! He also relished being seated next to the Head once he became the longest-living former pupil.

Hugh remained in close touch with his own Head, Sir James Cobban, whom he hugely respected. Hugh was very proud of his school and enjoyed returning to deliver lectures there. He also led a school expedition to the Himalayas and endowed a bursary for Abingdon's continued involvement with Asia.

From Sandhurst to Suez

The Royal Military Academy at Sandhurst was entirely Hugh's choice. His father had been in the First World War but did not particularly want Hugh to go into the army. He was, however, happy to endorse his son's choice.

Hugh spent eighteen months at Sandhurst, from September 1953 until commissioned in February 1955, aged twenty. He loved the place as, in his words 'it became "home" not having his own home'. His intake was No. 14, Normandy company, which he represented at soccer.

Despite being 'last in', Hugh managed to pass out rather higher up the pecking order 'at number one hundred – or was it one hundred and one but one person died – out of around two hundred and thirty' (of which some twenty-five were from overseas). He left with NQRA (not qualified Royal Artillery) after his name and didn't have the mathematical aptitude to go into the Royal Engineers. So it was that, although not really mechanical or technically minded, he chose the Tank Regiment. As he grew older, he found he liked striding across fields etc. and might have been, as he put it, a better infanteer but could not have been happier where he

2nd Lieutenant Leach, aged twenty, when first commissioned, February 1955.

was. The choice of the Tanks, plus the work of coincidence, shaped his life. If he had not made that choice, he would not have gone to Libya.

A fellow Royal Tank Regiment (RTR) officer, Martin Timmis, recalled in an obituary for *Tank*, the regiment's magazine, that Hugh passed out during the winter of 1955 with a commission into 6 RTR, which he duly joined in Münster, Germany. 'He made a somewhat inauspicious start to what he had hoped would be a successful military career when during his first duty as Regimental Orderly Officer he forgot his spectacles, without which he was as blind as a bat, and striding confidently through the barracks along with the Orderly Sergeant, he pulled up a tall figure and soundly berated him for failing to salute. The figure happened to be none other than the Commanding Officer, who duly apologised and promised to do better next time! It was well for Hugh that this particular officer had a sense of humour. Soon afterwards, the Regiment moved to Tidworth where Hugh continued to develop his troop-leading skills, as well as his obvious leadership qualities. Popular with his brother officers and soldiers alike, he was well respected by his troop, who developed a certain good-natured benevolence towards this rather eccentric officer of theirs!'

In July 1956, Egyptian leader Gamal Abdul Nasser nationalised the Suez Canal, previously controlled by Britain, which was freely open to traffic from

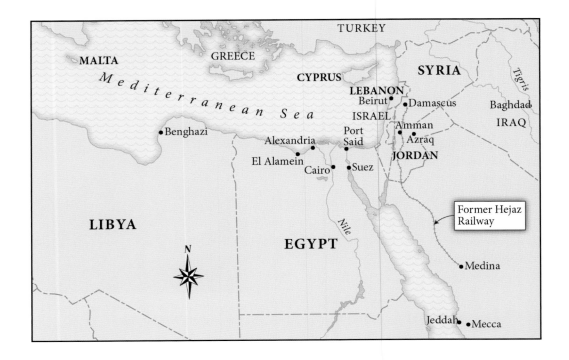

around the world. Britain, France and Israel secretly agreed that Israel would invade and seize the canal. The British and French would then intervene as peacekeepers and take back control. This happened, but, when Egypt refused to stop fighting, the RAF bombed Egypt's air force. With the USSR threatening to pitch in on the side of the Egyptians, the USA, who had no significant interest in the canal, used its political and financial power to order Britain and France to withdraw, a huge humiliation and a pivotal moment in modern British history.

Just before the Suez crisis began, Hugh, aged twenty-one, was briefly back in England, where he happened to be running a TA camp at Tilshead, on Salisbury Plain, living under canvas. The 6 RTR was chosen as a regiment to mobilise for the Suez operation. Hugh recalls having to find forty-seven Centurion tanks – quite a job. At the end of August, they set sail for Malta. No one on the island knew they were coming, so an entire regiment of tanks arrived on Malta in LSTs (Landing Ship, Tanks). They parked on a polo ground, living in tents and practising with the Marines for a possible landing at Suez. Was it on? Was it off?

HRL with his tank and crew.

It was on.

Before sailing for Egypt, the army had suggested that servicemen should write letters to their families. Hugh's letter to his father included the passage: 'I'm going to be perfectly all right because I have the best soldiers in the army with me and they will look after me and I will not be killed.'

They sailed from Malta in LCTs (Landing Craft, Tanks) which took a troop at a time, four tanks in a troop. It took about six days to Egypt, travelling day and night. There were to be no lights all the way until a Royal Marine fell off the front ship. Miraculously, he was picked up by the last one in the convoy, but all lights had to be turned on, which defeated the object of the blackout! (Ironically, unknown to the Allies, they had been tailed all the way by an American submarine.)

On 6 November, as dawn broke at 4.30 a.m off Port Said, Hugh looked out of the top of his tank and beheld the biggest flotilla since the war: seventy-two ships of the Anglo-French navies including the French battleship *Jean Bart* being used as a hospital ship. He said to himself, 'Leach, take a look at this, because it will never happen again'.

The night before, aircraft had bombed Nasser's airfields and, as Hugh's C Squadron disembarked, shells were flying over their tanks to land on the Egyptians. The squadron were to make a landing in twelve feet of water and the tanks had had their exhausts built up. However, as they hit *terra firma*, the built-up waterproof material that was all supposed to blow off at the push of a button was so wet that they had to get it off with crowbars.

Martin Timmis: 'Hugh's troop of tanks were the first ashore at Port Said... and were soon engaging the opposition around the area of the docks. Twice cut off from the Marines, Hugh on both occasions extricated his troop whilst under fire, with considerable coolness and tactical initiative. One incident involved a main armament engagement at close range with a truckload of drug-crazed fanatics; Hugh's laconic comment later was that there had been 'Conrods all over the place'. As a consequence of his actions that day he was recommended for an operational award.'

The invasion was a military success, but the Americans ordered that the action be halted. A fellow officer, Jeremy Williams, recalls: 'Hugh told me in Catterick that he was the lead troop leader in Centurions in 6 RTR during the Suez Canal crisis and that, had his radio not worked so that he could have not heard the Halt message, he'd have been right down the length of the canal! And never mind the American objections!'

Lieutenant Colonel Tom Gibbon, OBE, was his commanding officer at Suez and Hugh's greatest hero. Gibbon was one-armed and six feet five inches tall. He played polo with his one arm, having lost the other in the Second World War. Hugh really liked him: 'One of the most amazing and unusual officers – an officer's CO and a soldier's CO – he was both.' Hugh was later to spend several Christmases at Douneside House, Tarland in Scotland along with the Colonel.

Hugh kept his diary of Suez, which he said he probably should not have done. He had also very naughtily – his phrase – taken photos, the first operation he ever took part in. His album is, in his words: 'Probably one of the best photo albums of the Suez operation'. He presented this unique record to the Tank Museum in Dorset.

HRL with his troop at Suez. He would later reflect ruefully on their mission: 'I wake up at night sometimes – we must have killed fifty to sixty people on that operation'.

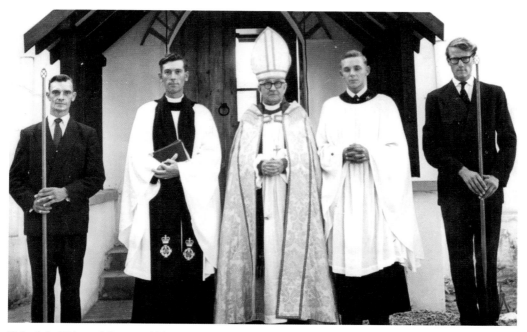

Visit of the Bishop of Egypt and Libya to 6 RTR at Al-Khums, for the dedication of the new garrison church. L-R: WO 2 Gordon Hocknell, Revd R T Wood, Chaplain to 6 RTR, Rt Revd F F Johnstone, Tpr Alan Dean, and Lt Hugh Leach.

After being among the first to land, Hugh's troop was among the last forces to depart, a month later, in time to reach Malta for Christmas.

Many years on, German diplomat Dr Werner Daum (now Professor) discussed Suez with Hugh: 'As a soldier, Hugh knew what war meant, in contrast to the politicians. He also disliked what he saw as Britain's self-subordination to the Americans…

'I asked him about his feelings during the Suez campaign, as reflected against his views as a mature person, and indeed, he put it down to his young age at the time. I then asked him what he would have done had he still been in active service in 2003? Hugh replied, "If you do not agree with your superiors, you have to remonstrate. If they stand by their orders, you may remonstrate once more, but you cannot do it a third time. Then you have to follow the orders." It was at this point where we disagreed — but of course, Hugh comes from another tradition, while I would see the moral issue from my German background.'

After Suez, Hugh went with the regiment to Libya for two years, punctuated by six months in Cyprus. The army were there to keep King Idris in power

HRL with Edwina in Wales on her sixtieth birthday tour, 1986.

EDWINA

Hugh's two great love affairs according to Paul Swift were Edwina and Martha 'who were, and remain, enduring symbols of Hugh's life'. Edwina was a 1926 vintage Humber 9/20 bought in 1957 on his return from Suez. For ten years, until Martha came on the scene, she was his only car (see Appendix B).

According to Martin Timmis, 'Hugh and a brother officer set about a complete refurbishment of the vehicle, spending every spare hour of the day and night doing so, until discovered by the Adjutant, and given a number of extra "Orderly Officers" for neglecting their regimental duties!'

In 2006, thirty-five guests attended Edwina's eightieth birthday party including the local vicar, who blessed the car. There was dancing to 1920s music played from her running board on a wind-up gramophone. Hugh sold the car in 2012 and wrote in the *Humber Register*: 'Yesterday was the saddest day of my seventy-eight years. Edwina, my 1926 Humber 9/20 Tourer, the nearest thing to a wife I've yet had, ran off with a younger man…' That man, Ian Coomber, kindly arranged for Edwina to be outside the church gate as Hugh left for his burial.

in Tobruk. It was during Hugh's time in Libya, and especially during his six months stationed at Al-Khums near Leptis Magna that, according to Martin Timmis, 'he became, in the immortal words of Walter de la Mare, "crazed with the spell of far Arabia"'.

Despite his experience in Suez, he little foresaw that he would spend the next thirty years in Arab countries. Interested in learning Arabic, Hugh found a local schoolteacher who came into the mess to teach him. This was considered deeply eccentric. However, as he was Assistant

HRL could ride, an ability which he modestly claimed got him into MECAS. This photograph shows him astride Nabil, 'the noble one', his horse during a later posting to Egypt.

Adjutant, across his desk came an annual Army Council Instruction calling for volunteers to learn languages. Hugh volunteered. His CO, Peter Vaux, was impressed: 'My boy,' he said, 'the Field Marshal's baton will drop out of your knapsack'.

Hugh was forced to admit that his previous qualifications for languages were sparse. Indeed, he was the only boy in the school to fail French oral in School Certificate. In desperation, the examiner had to break into English but she still ended up having to fail him. According to Hugh, she had never failed anyone before.

In view of this, Hugh was ordered to Tripoli to see a Major Sharpe, deputy in the Military Mission, who had completed a course at the Middle East Centre for Arab Studies (MECAS) in Lebanon. From Al-Khums, it was a seventy-mile trip in a jeep, which took up the morning. After lunch, Major Sharpe said 'I normally go for a ride after lunch. Do you ride?' Hugh did, and after a short horseback excursion, they went back for tea. At the time, there was a curfew as the locals were in the habit of stretching thin wires across the road to decapitate soldiers in jeeps. So, having tea, Hugh said, 'Sir, I really must leave as I have a two-hour drive back to Al-Khums'.

'Sorry about that,' replied Sharpe, 'but why did you come?'

'You are meant to be seeing me about Arabic.'

'Oh, you can ride a horse, so where is the form to sign?' And that was Hugh's account of how he got into MECAS.

AN ARABIST IS BORN

MECAS

In September 1958, Hugh began a ten-month intermediate Arabic course at the Middle East Centre for Arab Studies (MECAS) at Shemlan, a Lebanese village in the hills above Beirut. The college was run by the Foreign Office, most of the students being budding members of that department but with people like Hugh from other sources. The views were spectacular, but otherwise there was little to distract students from their learning.

The director was Donald Maitland (later Sir Donald), who became a lifelong friend. Most of the teaching staff were Arab. In the same intake as Hugh was Leslie McLoughlin, who later became Principal Instructor there. The course concentrated on modern literary Arabic, memorisation of word lists featuring prominently. Language-breaks were designed to give more exposure to spoken Arabic, if possible in a part of the Arab world where the individual student might later work.

Hugh chose Jordan for this break and for his first two weeks he was a schoolmaster there. The problem was that Arab boys wanted to speak English, and Hugh's Arabic didn't progress much. For his second location, Hugh opted for Azraq in north-east Jordan.

Opposite and above: HRL's home-made gateway to the Arabic language. On one side of a card was an English word, on the reverse its Arabic equivalent. Such was his interest in the language that he wrote an Omani Arabic dictionary after his two-year assignment in Nizwa.

T. E. Lawrence had been based there briefly in November 1917 during the First World War. This time, to Hugh's advantage, everyone there spoke only Arabic.

Donald Maitland had instructed students not to travel in or linger in Syria, but on their return journeys, both Hugh and a fellow student, Ken Urquhart, ended up in Damascus en route back to Shemlan. They were given a rocket, but Hugh's Arabic continued to improve.

We can see why from this golden 'Hugh' experience contributed by Guy Burn: 'I arrived to live in Amman towards the end of 1958. About a month later the Italian Chargé d'Affaires' son and I decided to go and see Damascus. I was nearly eighteen and Francesco a similar age. Old Damascus is very dramatic, being mostly of black basalt with many of the streets roofed over. I saw an "interesting", dark, possibly fierce, street. I was about to go down it, Francesco being thirty or forty yards away, when a really scruffy evil-looking beggar began pestering me…"*Ana miskin, jib faloos*…etc.," *Allah* imprecations, and more. As I was trying to turn away from him he came right up beside my ear and said in clear 'officer' tones, "I wouldn't go down there if I were you, old chap!" He was gone immediately.

'Years later, now knowing Hugh quite well, I wondered if he had been that beggar, and ventured to ask. Of course, it was him!'

At the end of the MECAS course Maitland was encouraging: Hugh would be eligible to join the advanced course if and when the army approved. However, Hugh was required elsewhere and he returned to Kent to take a four-month course at the Army Intelligence Corps training centre. Hugh was not to return to MECAS for over two years.

Desert Intelligence Officer

In 1962 Hugh wrote in the *Griffen*, the magazine of the Old Abingdonian Club, 'Muscat and Oman are countries which I should have had difficulty in finding in an atlas whilst I was at school: still less should I ever have connected them with a military career I was then contemplating. However, in less than eight years of leaving school I was to find myself employed in the somewhat romantic sounding role of a 'Desert Intelligence Officer' in just that country.

'There is little room in an article of this length to describe the political back-ground which has led up to recent events in Eastern Arabia. Suffice it to say that the successive Sultans of Muscat have always claimed that they held

Nizwa Fort painted in 1961 by Andrew Johnstone. HRL chose to live in a mud-built house near the fort, well away from the army camp, for the two years he was in Oman, 1959–61.

sway over both the coastal regions of Muscat and Dhofar as well as the more mountainous and inaccessible regions of the interior of Oman Proper. Such a claim has invariably been disputed by the Imam of Oman, a religious leader elected by the tribes of the interior, who have considered that they held complete autonomy. In 1955 the matter was put to the test by a recently elected Imam, Ghalib bin Ali, led by his more ambitious brother Talib, openly rebelling against the authority of the Sultan. The latter reminded the British Government of its treaty obligations, doubtless concluded in a more gracious and imperial age, and with some reluctance they finally ejected this recalcitrant upstart Ghalib from the top of the Jebel Akhdar, or Green Mountain, from where he made his final stand in early 1959. The Imam and his kinsmen found a benevolent if not somewhat flattering host in Saudi Arabia from where they settled down to organise a running fight against the Sultan and his locally raised forces.

'This was still the status quo when I arrived in Muscat on what was an extremely hot and sticky day in mid-winter 1959...How well I remember lying off what has often been described as one of the most picturesque harbours in the world thinking that no one could possibly look at that dark mysterious coastline without wanting to find out what lay behind.

'My wish was soon granted for I was to make my base in the town of Nizwa, which lay some ninety miles into the interior at the feet of the Jebel Akhdar and was the very seat of the deposed Imam himself. I decided that, since it was my job to find out what was going on, I should be in the centre of things and therefore I moved into one of the local mud houses in the town. I don't suppose I shall ever live in such unconventional surroundings again. There was little furniture in the house; the floor served the treble purpose of bed, chair and table. Sanitation was simply a question of "the desert's a large place". A permanent hot bath was provided by a system of underground water courses known as *falajes*. One such was just outside my front door and its entrance was like that of a tube station. Food was either by courtesy of one of Mr Heinz's 57 Varieties or locally bought goat and rice. The latter was cheaper and more enjoyable. I recruited a local Arab crew and paid them from a sack of Maria Theresa dollars, large silver *thalers* of Austrian origin introduced into the country in the 18th century. Although there was a camp of the Sultan's armed forces nearby outside the town, my main communication with the outside world was by means of a radio worked by an Arab signaller, who could neither speak nor read English, but knew how to translate English hieroglyphics into morse and vice versa.'

The article continued: 'The people of Oman are from an extremist offshoot of Islam known as *Ibadhiya*. They are renowned for their dislike of foreigners, particularly Christians.* Until the present crisis only a handful of Europeans had set foot in the country. My job of course entailed getting to know and enjoy the confidence of the people and in particular their sheiks and leaders. I was equipped with two Land Rovers and the majority of time was spent out travelling. I would have occasion to go as far north as Buraimi and the Trucial

*As his posting was six decades ago, Hugh would probably recast the description of *Ibadhiya* in his article differently were he writing it now, to reflect changed conditions and perceptions of Oman since 1962. It may also be helpful to set his posting in a wider historical framework. At the time of Hugh's posting to Nizwa, Britain retained strategic military interests east of the Suez Canal and, although Oman was an independent Sultanate, British and Omani military structures were closely inter-related. A priority for British officers and their counterparts in the Omani forces (some of whom were British contract officers) was to monitor and quell any remaining armed rebel activity after the so-called 'Jebel Akhdar War'. Prevention of any residual rebel mine-laying capacity was particularly important during this tail-end of the war. Previous SAS action to reach the top of the difficult terrain had turned the tables in favour of the Sultan. As a result of steady military vigilance, the Sultan's authority became visibly established in areas of the interior. Before then, central government from Muscat or from the Sultan's residence in Salala in Dhofar, had been for the most part symbolic.

States [modern day UAE] on the Persian Gulf coast. Much has been written in romantic vein about the "desert and the stars" – it's all true! The joy of spending nights in utter solitude or with the Bedouin must be among the most rewarding things in life. The inner mountains were of course traversed by foot. It is remarkable to think that a mountain range of 10,000 feet exists in Arabia. The villages on top are inhabited by a most remarkable in-bred society and such lush fruits as pomegranates and peaches are found growing there.

'At the end of my two years in Muscat and Oman I found I had become remarkably fond of the people. Despite their supposed hostility towards Christians, their hospitality and manners made one feel ashamed of one's own Western coarseness. One realised that here was a people who had still been little influenced by outside society but even this was changing all too fast with the search for oil at full pace, with all its attendant vulgarities.

'I think I can best describe the outlook on life of a typical Omani by reciting a small incident. One day I was with one of my Arab companions watching some "Baluch" soldiers of the Sultan's forces playing football in the nearby camp. I turned to him and said, "Well what do you think of that as a game?" His face was one of complete disgust. "By God what a waste – they're neither killing each other nor making any money out of it." Maybe he had something!'

Ivor Lucas wrote of this time: 'Hugh Leach was a very dear friend and a greatly-admired member of that bevy of skilled operators who plied their trade mainly in the mountains and deserts of Oman and the area known in the 1950s as the Trucial States. [During this period, the Buraimi Oasis north of Nizwa had been a thorny regional issue] Six of the nine villages in the oasis were claimed (against the Saudis) by Shaikh Shakhbut of Abu Dhabi and the other three by the Sultan of Oman. British help rendered by the Trucial Oman Scouts / Levies was instrumental in upholding the interest of both Shakhbut and the Sultan.'

After the operational requirements had subsided, Hugh later received a wooden chest as a gift from the brother of Salah bin Issa, one of the four rebel leaders. The rebels received support, including firearms, from Saudi Arabia, and it was to Dammam, in the Eastern Province of Saudi Arabia, that Salah bin Issa eventually escaped and took refuge. The chest must have been a wry reminder of Hugh's contribution to tracking and countering previous rebel activity, whose forms included mine-laying and targeting Omanis loyal to Sultan Sa'id bin Taimur as well as British officers. Indeed, Radio Cairo (supportive to the rebels) reported more than once the death of the British officer Hugh Leach

– inaccurately as Hugh gleefully attested – but it was evidence that even at the tail end of the Jebel Akhdar war, it had its dangers. Once, when he was away from the dwelling he rented in Nizwa, his Adeni signaller, sleeping on the roof, narrowly escaped death from a bullet probably intended for Hugh.

General Sir Robert Pascoe, then a young Captain, had met Hugh for the first time in 1957 at MECAS. The General reports that, on one occasion when staying with him at his house on the outskirts of Nizwa, 'we heard shots some way off and Hugh dismissed this as some form of local celebration and nothing to worry about or investigate. Sometime later I read a resumé of a Radio Cairo report that said that Captain Leach had been killed, and the date of the alleged attack matched that of the shooting we had heard. This was but one of three such false claims put out by Radio Cairo during Hugh's time in Nizwa. Hugh's house lacked a bathroom so we used to take a dip in a nearby open *falaj*, waiting until dusk before stripping off and immersing our bodies in the clear waters, where little fish nibbled gently at our toes.'

These were, despite the risks, happy days in Hugh's memory. Although he was an officer in the Sultan's armed forces, he was also part of the British army and a member of a small network of similar officers who contributed information to a centre in Bahrain. He liked the local people of Nizwa and enjoyed living away from a central base.

According to Bill Woodburn, an army officer on secondment to the Trucial Oman Scouts: 'He really got immersed in the local scene...There was one occasion when Hugh, after making endless fuss at the very highest levels about the clapped-out state of his vehicles, collected two brand-new Land Rovers from Sharjah. Driving back to Nizwa Hugh, in the leading vehicle, had to brake hard in a cloud of dust. His cook (typical Hugh set-up) was driving in the second Land Rover far too close and

Shisham wood chest given to HRL by the brother of Salah bin Issa, one of the rebel leaders in Oman.

HRL cuts a distinctive figure in the streets of Oman.

went straight into the back of Hugh's. Both vehicles were written off. A furious Hugh, but the rest of us could not resist a chuckle.' Even Hugh admitted that the debacle took place where there was room enough for a thousand Land Rovers to drive side by side.

Indeed, life overseas with Hugh was rarely without incident. James Johnstone recalled how on one occasion '...when out duck shooting in some dark marsh in Arabia, Hugh accidentally shot my father, Andrew, in the face and didn't believe it when Andrew told him so. It was only when they returned to their Land Rover that Hugh saw that Andrew's face was covered in blood and full of pellets, and he was mortified. For them, that seems to have been a typical day out.'

Martin Timmis summarises Hugh's time in Oman: it was 'as Hugh readily admitted, the most enjoyable of his Army career and after which he was awarded the MBE (Mil) for his outstanding intelligence work in combating the Omani rebel threat at that time. Indeed, his flawless command of Arabic, his unique knowledge of Oman and its people, as well as the threat within that country had made him a leading regional expert in his own right.' As Hugh wrote, 'Lying under the stars at night I would think: "Not only am I doing this, someone is paying me for it!" How lucky we were…'

In December 1961, at the end of his posting to Nizwa, he returned to MECAS where he completed the last two months of the Advanced Course and passed, qualifying him at the level of an interpreter. The following year marked his election in July to membership of the Royal Central Asian Society, as the Royal Society for Asian Affairs was then known, proposed by Tom Walcot, a fellow Tank Regiment officer, and seconded by Group Captain Harold St Clair Smallwood, Honorary Secretary of the Society.

Back to Catterick

After MECAS, Hugh transferred in 1962 to Catterick, served as 2 I/C to a squadron and then as Adjutant to the 3rd Royal Tank Regiment.

Colonel Bruce Duncan recollects that: 'Hugh was a good friend to me (and later Toni) when we served together in Catterick in 1962–4; he was the Adjutant, whilst I was a subaltern. We both owned old cars; his was a 1926 Humber…and mine was a 1934 Aston Martin Mk2. We used to work on these vehicles together in an old Nissen hut on camp…

'Hugh was clearly an eccentric and would sometimes take parades wearing jodhpurs and riding boots with his service dress, some forty or more years after this ceased to be our Regiment's correct order of dress. But Hugh could carry it off and not even the RSM had the courage to challenge him on the matter!

'One day he laughingly told me that when taking Guard Mounting Parade at night, the Orderly Officer could bark out anything and the Parade would react automatically to execute the correct drill movement. I decided to give it a go! The correct words of command were: "Guard Commander…Take Post!" I gave the order "Guard Commanders…Make Toast!" The drill movement was carried out perfectly and I smiled quietly to myself as I marched off parade, only to see Hugh standing at the edge of the square. He was not amused and told me never to do that again. But, being utterly fair, and realising he was partly to blame, he left it at that rather than give me the dozen or so extra Orderly Officer duties I deserved.'

Jeremy Williams, says: 'One evening he invited a few young officers including me to go with him in his own Land Rover (no one else had one!) to a play in Newcastle, which we did. On the way back, on the A1, with large vehicles all around us, he pulled into a lay-by and there, traffic right next to us, in the gloom and slight rain of an evening on the A1, he laid out a carpet in the lay-by and proceeded to serve us coffee in little cups. In those days, I had absolutely no idea of the significance of this Arab hospitality – we all thought him completely mad, but in a nice way!'

Guy Burn adds: 'At Catterick we'd quite often be sitting round after dinner when the Infantry half a mile away would play Last Post: Adjutant Leach would say, "Fall-in Outside!" and we, the young officers present, would go out and line up. Adjutant Leach would play Last Post back at the Infantry, infinitely more competently, on his Frontier Force bugle with its exceptional tone.'

One awkwardness Hugh faced was that this appointment came at a particularly difficult time for the regiment. As Adjutant, he had to employ diplomatic skills which would later stand him in good stead.

But the powers-that-be recognised that these skills, together with Hugh's Arabic knowledge, would be better employed abroad.

From Yorkshire to the Yemen

The reputation that Hugh had gained from his counter-insurgency work in Oman led to his secondment in 1963 as a Political Officer in the (British) West Aden Protectorate abutting the independent Yemeni state to the north. In 1962 it had become the Yemen Arab Republic (YAR).

Before this time, northern Yemen had been ruled by a monarchical Imamate on traditional lines. It had never come under a colonial administration. Events in Egypt, particularly Suez in 1956, had fuelled regional Arab nationalist and republican feeling and when Imam Ahmad, who had ruled since 1948, died in September 1962, his son Muhammad Al-Badr was opposed by military officers. Muhammad rallied support in the north of the country but the new government in Sana'a sought and received military support from Nasserist Egypt. The Egyptian aims were both to strengthen establishment of a republic in YAR and to oust Britain from its position in Aden and its hinterland to the south. Within the YAR, conflict continued between the government's forces and residual royalist supporters whose support for that cause continued until the end of the decade.

HRL with Yemeni tribesmen.

For its part, Britain adjusted the colonial status of the city of Aden, which ceased to be a colony governed directly from London via the Colonial Office and was attached instead to a loose 'Federation of South Arabia' composed of areas run mainly by tribal and family groupings. Rugged, mountainous terrain intensified local loyalties and posed difficulties to any administration from Aden. Ruling families for the most part judged it in their interest to continue to co-operate with Britain, but opposition to a continuing British presence grew and took form in two organisations, the National Liberation Front (NLF) and the Front for the Liberation of South Yemen (FLOSY). The administration in Aden wished to forestall either of these organisations from drawing cross-border support from the YAR. It was feared that Egyptian forces in the YAR, who numbered at one stage up to 70,000, could increase the capacity of those ready to use violence in a campaign to 'decolonise' all of Yemen.

Hugh was assigned to the area of Mukairas in the Western Aden Protectorate. There, the mountain plateau was over 6,000 feet above sea-level. He was to monitor any attempts from the YAR to infiltrate this area in order to undermine security within the Federation. He had command of a detachment of (Baluch) troops in a role that bridged the political and military and included intelligence-gathering. Activity along the frontier came to be termed a 'jebel war' and included British fatalities. Such a working environment called for courage and astute risk-taking. Hugh proved he had both qualities in abundance. It was not always orthodox or deadly serious, however, as recounted by John Malcolm and Alun Evans.

John lets Hugh tell the story: 'We were under constant but sporadic rifle fire from the Yemenis on the other side of the valley. But the bullets never actually seemed to hit anyone. One day an aide rushed into my office and announced that a small party of Yemenis had descended from their side of the hill and were advancing across the valley, carrying a white flag. I immediately left my office and dashed down to the valley. "Have you come to surrender?" I cried. "Well, no, actually. The fact is that we have run out of ammunition and can't keep up the fire on your position, which we have been ordered to do. Could you possibly lend us a few hundred rounds so that we can fulfil our orders?"' Alun added, 'The answer, it being Hugh, was "Yes"'.

At one stage, Hugh became interested in another type of cross-border activity. He learned that old British army uniforms were available on sale on the other side of the border in Beidha Suq, inside YAR. He managed to get hold of 150 of them, packed in corded bales. They had perhaps been stored at the Tel El Kebir depot in Egypt, looted after Suez and passed on by Egyptian troops to North Yemeni allies.

Some years later, uniforms from this trove were used for display by soldiers marching during the Trooping the Colour ceremony. An article in the *Daily Telegraph* drew attention to the use

HRL's bodyguard in South Yemen wearing Coldstream Guards' uniforms he had acquired. Believed to have been looted after Suez, they were passed on by Egyptian troops to their North Yemeni allies.

of old army uniforms without further explanation of where and how they came from. Hugh himself frequently retold the story, with enjoyment.

Sultana Al-Quaiti mentions that her husband Ghalib's friendship with Hugh went back to 1967. 'Hugh,' she says, 'was one of the first to join Friends of Hadhramaut in 1996 and remained an ardent supporter.'

Hugh's service in the West Aden Protectorate was not part of an orthodox military career and he increasingly faced a dilemma whether to continue along a military path or to transfer into the British Foreign Service. With his track record and his Arabic language skills, he had been attracted and encouraged to transfer, but at the same time he had loved his army life and the military *esprit de corps*. By his own admission, he experienced real turmoil in coming to a decision. Martin Timmis says: 'Hugh genuinely enjoyed the Army, its customs, its traditions and above all the comradeship, so one can only imagine the agonising he endured.'

As with so many lives, Hugh's future pivoted on a small moment. At an advanced stage in preparing to leave the Army, he had a change of mind and set out to travel to the War Office to renounce his decision. By chance he encountered his former CO at Catterick and explained his predicament. The colonel persuaded Hugh to stick to his choice of foreign service, for which his talents were so well suited. Hugh was forever grateful to him for this chance, crucial advice. He met the entry exam requirements and due weight was given to his qualifications from MECAS. So it was that, in 1967, Hugh joined the Foreign Office.

A silver dagger, inscribed: 'This Yemeni *jambia* is presented to the officers of the 3rd Royal Tank Regiment by Captain H. R. Leach MBE in appreciation of the tolerance shown by a succession of Commanding Officers in allowing him to serve for many years away from the Regiment in Arabia. February 1966.'

Opposite: Captain H. R. Leach, MBE. A portrait from his final years in the Army.

DIPLOMATIC SERVICE

Saudi Arabia and Jordan

In 1967 Hugh was posted as Second Secretary and Vice Consul to the British Embassy in Saudi Arabia, located at that time in Jeddah on the Red Sea. During 1967, one result of the British withdrawal from southern Yemen was an exodus of traditional local rulers who had previously judged that it was advantageous for them to remain close to the British administration. Not a few became exiles in the Kingdom of Saudi Arabia, for whom upheavals in north and south Yemen were, and are, an ongoing concern.

Cooling off in the desert. HRL relaxes on one of his many excursions with Martha.

A lifelong camper, Hugh had wide scope for travel across the Saudi kingdom and as far as Dhahran on the Gulf, and took full advantage of this licence. Not that travel was easy: at that time there was no tarmac road beyond Taif to Riyadh and it took three days to travel across the country. Luckily, Hugh had Martha.

Ann Ward recalls a journey with Hugh up into the mountains of Saudi Arabia: 'I had grown up in New Zealand...and had no idea about the Arab world and their culture and I had never heard of Islam. I had been to a strict Roman Catholic boarding school, which was also a

Opposite: A village of the Saudi Asir (near Bil Jarashi).

convent where young nuns were trained, so that helped me to cope with all the restrictions of life in the royal households in Jeddah and Riyadh. But I did not realise that going on a trip alone with Hugh would cause a lot of comment in the royal family, an indication of my scanty understanding of the local culture. Hugh must have known that it would attract attention, but, as many know, he was his own man!'

A small section of Hejaz Railway track which he preserved and made into a bookend.

Hugh took every opportunity to follow the line of the old Ottoman Hejaz Railway northwards from Medina and built up a vivid and extensive collection of photographs of engines, long abandoned in the sand, now in the Imperial War Museum.

Martin Timmis recalls accompanying Hugh on a similar journey along the railway route, and particularly remembers 'being subjected each day, in the middle of absolutely nowhere, to his customary Last Post and Reveille bugle calls.'

Anna Vaudrey (née Harris) went on a journey to the railway with Hugh and Robbie Begbie, the son of the Defence Attaché, and remembers 'three days camping under the stars, exploring stations and swimming in murky pools, ignoring possible bilharzia. Having visited trains blown-up by Lawrence during the day, at night we read out loud *The Seven Pillars of Wisdom*. With the temperature at 120°F, it was pure joy when it rained on our final day and we all jumped out of the vehicle to cool down in the storm. In true Hugh fashion, we sang hymns as we drove.'

The only thing Anna could remember eating was Hugh's cucumber soup. He also insisted that both his young passengers should keep a log of their travels. Hugh's spell in Saudi Arabia was interrupted in 1970 by an interim posting to Amman, where he

One of HRL's collection of photographs of the abandoned Ottoman Hejaz Railway.

MARTHA

Hugh bought Martha, a Series IIA Land Rover, new from Solihull in 1967. Four miles after leaving the factory, her speedometer failed and he had to return to have it replaced. She never failed him again, even winning the 'In Search of a Legend' competition celebrating fifty years of Land Rover in 1998. The search was for a vehicle '…with the most unique qualities of freedom, adventure, and individualism, authenticity and guts…', all qualities Hugh admired in Martha.

Hugh's wonderful entry says as much about his own story as about Martha's: 'I was cast specially in my mother's womb at Solihull for arduous duties in the East. Just as well, for in long and hard diplomatic postings in Saudi Arabia, Egypt, Yemen and the Sudan, I explored every corner of those countries. I have crossed many deserts including the Great Nefud, forded rivers and often driven along the old Hejaz Railway wrecked by T. E. Lawrence. I've had adventures in Jordan, Syria, Lebanon, Iraq, Kuwait, Iran, Afghanistan and Pakistan. I've been in wars, insurrections and coups d'etat. I've been shot at, held up at gun point, escaped from kidnapping and confronted rioting mobs. I have carried Princes and Princesses, Vice-Presidents and Prime Ministers. I've camped with many a famous explorer including Sir Wilfred Thesiger and Dame Freya Stark. And so much more but alas, like my owner, I've signed the Official Secrets Act, so I must leave the rest to your imagination...

'I should add that I've never let my owner down in all those quarter of a million miles. Plenty of punctures yes, but Land Rover don't make tyres! And he's looked after me pretty well – doing all the servicing and minor repairs himself and never letting anyone else drive me.'

Martin Timmis adds that Hugh's prize 'was the company's most recent model of Land Rover Defender. He never drove it!'

HUGH'S RECIPE FOR ARABIAN *MANSAF*

Leg or shoulder of lamb, goat or gazelle

4oz rice per person (white Basmati is good)

Quantity of sultanas (golden are best), pine nuts,
flaked almonds, any other nuts

Dates, salt, saffron, dried rosemary or mint

1 each of red, yellow and green pepper

Moonlit night…

Cut off excess fat from meat and cook for 1½ to 2 hours, or until tender. An ideal method is to cook in a terracotta 'brick'. When cooked drain off the juices into a basin.

Take 4oz of rice per person (on assumption guests have hollow legs). Put twice the volume of rice to water into a pan and bring to the boil. Add two pinches of saffron and salt to taste. Cook rice for approximately 15 minutes (longer if brown). Transfer to a steamer for a further 5–10 minutes to 'fluff' out. Mix in the sultanas, which have previously been placed in near boiling water for 15 minutes, and the nuts. Put the rice and ingredients onto a large open charger and place in the oven on a low temperature.

Cut the meat into small cubes and the peppers into small pieces and mix into the rice. Alternatively put the meat on top. Place the dates round the edge of the charger.

Now carry the charger into the garden where oriental rugs have been spread out, and a full moon is in the heavens. Sit cross-legged and eat with the right hand only. Starting with the dates. Imagine you are in the Great Nefud Desert in northern Arabia or part of a Pasolini film-set for the Arabian Nights. For the faint-hearted, place the charger on the dining room table and eat in the normal way. If there are left-overs, it freezes well or may be eaten on the following day. In the latter event, remove the set meat fat from the juices in the basin and pour the heated jelly over the rice.

I enjoy this recipe because it reminds me of Arabian days.
Hugh. Choumert Square, 2008

stood in for a member of the Embassy on compassionate leave at home. This was a troubled year for Jordan, as tensions between Palestinian organisations and the Jordanian host country led to the civil war known as 'Black September'. Not that the troubles were constant. As Peter Clark's anecdote illustrates, there was scope for partying: 'In 1970, a junior secretary at the Embassy was due to leave and Hugh organised a farewell party. It was held in the ruins of the palace at Mshatta, the Umayyad desert fort a few miles south of the Jordanian capital. We all gathered in the ruins and when a *mansaf*, lamb piled on rice seasoned with pine-nuts, was brought in, Hugh appeared on the battlements summoning us to eat with his bugle call. What a farewell party!'

A Place of His Own
'Something Out of the Ordinary'

In the course of changing direction in career, Hugh also decided that it was timely to find a place to stay in London. A property advertisement in the *Sunday Times* caught his eye because it contained the phrase '…if you want something out of the ordinary'. He went to view 21 Choumert Square in Peckham Rye and fell in love with it, buying it for £2,900, with the help of a £1,000 loan. He set about getting a fireplace installed and himself built in cupboards and bookshelves. Hugh rated himself as a good 'chippy'.

He was described as being: '…a very clubbable but also very private man in many ways. His cottage, one of a row of early Victorian workers' cottages in South London, was an appropriately modest yet most distinctive home, as unusual and special as he was.' In the not-infrequent articles in the national press and magazines about Choumert Square, Hugh invariably had a mention.

Hugh loved the rich multi-cultural mix in Peckham and, after his postings abroad, settled easily back in Choumert Square and resumed local friendships. After one such return from abroad, he overheard two little boys, who lived in a nearby road, calling out 'Mum, Hughie's back!'.

Among his range of interests, Hugh was very keen on astronomy; one of his delights was to take the children of a local Indian shopkeeper to the suitably dark nearby car park and teach them the constellations.

Keith Hamilton and Graham Reuby, later to be neighbours at Hugh's Somerset home, '…never knew him to lock his door, day or night; he was touchingly trusting that people would be kind to him and good. He never tired of saying

Number 21 Choumert Square, Peckham, before (1969) and during (2008) HRL's residence there. The distinctive roundels remained throughout.

that he was an Arab and that as such his door was always open and that he would take it as an insult if you telephoned or knocked and asked if you could call in.'

Rebecca Wilmshurst contributes this charming recollection of Hugh's life in Choumert Square: 'Even the most spirited adventurer returns to his home. And for almost half a century, Hugh's London home was Choumert Square in Peckham – an urban microcosm of Hugh's wider world. He was comfortable here and on easy-speaking terms (often in the native tongue) with everyone: tradesmen, people running local shops, cafes, restaurants, the launderette, the cinema, the mosque. It's a community where he could most contentedly blend in and show us all not only his remarkable talent for friendship but his humanity. And he was hugely loved by us all.

'At the heart of his London life was the little house to which he'd welcome friends from every corner of his world. You approached it down a surprisingly leafy inner city laneway, through a tinkling garden gate under an arch of Handel roses. His front door intriguingly bore an inscription in Arabic. A key would turn twice within a lion's head key fob, and then – you entered an entirely magical setting! His home bore all the trappings of a lifetime's scholarship – yet these sat easily in the haven of tranquil comfort that he'd lovingly created. And all to the gentle ticking of a wall-clock that belied the fact that Time, as well as Care, seemed here to have no place.

'Whenever Hugh returned from his travels to the Square, people suddenly and strangely felt more secure. Everything was back in its rightful place, a sense that "all was well". More prosaically, his presence promised us endless kitchen

One wall of 21 Choumert Square says everything about the occupant's love of books and his rich collection of pictures and photographs.

coffee conversations, or shared wisdom over chicken-brick suppers! When I think of Hugh now, it's no surprise that I think first not of desert kingdoms but of the London home he loved so much. I smile to remember those wonderfully idiosyncratic habits of his domestic life: the way, in his smoking days, he'd enjoy a pipe by a roaring log fire disregarding the sparks it jettisoned across his beautiful Kashmiri carpets; how he'd boil an egg, timing it exactly to two verses of "Onward Christian Soldiers" (his Aunt Theodora's schooling), terrifying onlookers by scooping the eggs from the boiling water with his bare hands; the joy with which he'd settle into a *Just William* story. And his own schoolboy delight as he'd set off on a favourite excursion – I think of trips to Zippo's Circus, the excitement he'd fire in companions on the way to the Big Top, to be followed – in no set order – by the utter contentment of a glass of claret in the Circus Master's waggon or the flourish of a sticky wand of candyfloss at the ringside, or the childlike thrill equally lavished on watching daredevil trapeze artists or a troupe of brave little budgies performing tricks on command. I recall the way tears would well up if he caught the sound of a brass band playing a favourite hymn or carol, or after reading a much-loved poem that had especially moved him.

'Though a country man at heart, he relished his urban seasons. His Springtime garden makeover for the Square's annual NGS Open Day was always preceded by an early delivery of plants from the local nursery (where he was affectionately known as The General) before he'd tackle the planting operation in full overalls over four pints of tea. When at home, his

Rebecca Wilmshurst plays the harmonium at 21 Choumert Square. Christmas, 2004.

summer afternoons might be spent happily sipping wine with visiting friends either in the communal garden, or inside the garden arbour he'd created in the tiny space between his garden gate and front-door. He'd insist on a daily walk and his favourite autumn stroll (seven miles!) was over One Tree Hill, where, if Fate was on his side, he'd find logs to carry home loudly singing "Good King Wenceslas" – his own "take" on gathering winter fuel now complete. Once home, a fire would soon blaze in the Georgian grate and if you were lucky, there'd be butter-dripping toasted crumpets spread thick with Marmite and endless servings of tea in blue Spode cups. Evening supper would be preceded by a small whisky and perhaps a glass or two of a Berry Brothers choice red wine. Winter was his cinema season – Hugh especially loved old black and white films: a favourite was Hitchcock's *The Lady Vanishes*. Once I took him to see *The Shop Around the Corner* – as "THE END" appeared, the cinema emptied; but Hugh sat in a motionless trance, strangely stirred by the simplicity and beauty of the film's message. On really frosty winter nights Hugh would lead young friends to the car park and, as ringmaster to the cosmos, gently show and introduce them to the stars.

'Every December Hugh would lead the Choumert Square Carols, an event he began in the early 1980s and which we continue in his honour. I shared many Christmas Days with Hugh – once the feasting was done in one house, he'd like nothing better than to return to his own, light the fire, and invite everyone in. Dinner would always be followed by carols around his beloved harmonium. My last meal with Hugh was on Christmas Day 2013 – and there was no sign of his imminent decline: indeed, he was on sparkling form and perfect company as I stood by his front door and said goodnight.

'And of that Arabic inscription? Oddly, I never asked him what it meant. But when the time came to sell his house, the new owner told me it translated as 'Hello and welcome'. That simple statement is redolent of the Hugh I'll remember: a very special gentleman who, in all circumstances, was always ready to meet, greet and reach out to his fellow man and, as befits a gracious host, to offer them a welcome to his world that they would never forget.'

Return to Jeddah

By January 1971, Hugh was back in Jeddah, now as First Secretary and Vice Consul. The Ambassador at this time was Willie Morris (later Sir Willie Morris KCMG). Relations with the Yemen Arab Republic (YAR) had improved sufficiently for Morris to be accredited to the YAR also, as an interim measure. He assigned two of his staff (Christopher Gandy and Hugh) to assist with travel arrangements. Hugh travelled with two embassy Land Rovers from Jeddah to Sana'a. Willie Morris and his family flew to Sana'a for the presentation of credentials but, for the return journey, Hugh took them all by land on an expedition through the mountains back to Jeddah. Willie's son Peter continues the story:

'Hugh Leach must have entranced hundreds, if not thousands, of children over the course of his life. I and my two brothers were lucky enough to be three of them. In January 1971, when we were seven, eight and ten, we travelled overland from Sana'a to Jeddah with Hugh. Naturally the bugle that sat on the pulpit at Hugh's memorial service came along, too.

'Along the way, we would take the opportunity to meet some of the tiny number of British nationals working in Yemen…We headed up into the mountains along roads that in those days were often no more than tracks. Hugh had assured [our mother] Ghislaine there would be no need for tents. But the night we spent out in the open at 6,500 feet, when the thermometer showed 41 degrees Fahrenheit in the morning, went down in family legend as the Coldest Ever. Luckily, Hugh was there to keep three small boys entertained…The next night we made sure to find a simple hotel where we all slept on the floor but in the dry and warm. In all, this memorable trip from Sana'a to Jeddah took about eight days.'

During his journeys in Saudi Arabia, Hugh collected plants for the Natural

HRL on official business in Saudi Arabia with the Ambassador, Willie Morris (right), and unidentified colleagues.

On the journey from Sana'a to Jeddah, Peter Morris, his brothers and the group's two drivers are entertained by HRL who 'sounded Reveille too, but perhaps no one was up early enough to get a picture of that!'

History Museum. He had a particular fascination with biblical plants and admitted that he rather wished to have had one named after him. Once 'in Amman, he was captured by brigands while laying vole traps on a visit to the Karak Hills but charmed his way free after two days...Over the years of his service, he was an avid plant collector.'

Hugh continued to travel and camp extensively in Saudi Arabia until the end of his posting. Of the years he spent there – four in total – he reckoned that he had slept out one night in four.

A boy in the Sinai Peninsula holding a specimen of *Anastatica hierochuntica* (Rose of Jericho), one of several hundred plants HRL collected for the Natural History Museum.

Additionally, with relevant clearances, he had also made unusual journeys outside the Kingdom.

In early 1971, he travelled from Tehran to a remote area of Luristan in north-west Iran with some members of the British Embassy and an Iranian military captain provided as an escort. Sarah Biffen was part of the expedition and says: 'After a tediously long drive from Tehran, the party eventually set off on an extremely arduous and muddy walk in the March rain...the sort of mud that builds up on your boots, getting heavier and heavier before eventually dropping off, and a repeat of the process. I was five months pregnant with my daughter Lucy and a few hours of this just about finished me. A mule was found and I continued. After endless miles we eventually arrived at a village near a river where we were to stay the night. An appalling rubber chicken was slaughtered in our honour. Next morning a crisis meeting convened as we surveyed the river, a raging torrent swelled with the spring rains. Normally, a raft made of inflated goat skins would have carried us across, but last year's goat skins were cracked and unusable. Gloom descended. However, undaunted, after a short delay Hugh was last seen mounted on an Arab stallion accompanied by a nervous soldier triumphantly swimming across the river. Successfully reaching the other side, with a wave he was off...and that was the last time I saw him for forty years!'

Hugh told vivid tales of Luristan's animal perils. One night the camp was invaded by a pack of wolves. All one could do, he said, was to lie silent in the tent, hoping fervently that they would pass. Their ferocity was only matched by the huge and ubiquitous sheepdogs of the region which posed a similar threat to life and limb. According to Hugh, 'the general technique to pass by them without being savaged seems to be to throw some huge rock at the brutes, which they will bound after in fury, and satisfy themselves by sharpening their teeth on this instead of yourself.'

In May 1971, Hugh obtained permission to fly into the YAR to visit the remote town of Sa'dah, a place which had been rarely visited by European travellers and in which, according to representatives of the exiled Royalist government, there remained some of an ancient Yemeni Jewish community. These reports ran counter to claims that the entire Jewish population had transferred to Israel in the years 1948–51, under 'Operation Magic Carpet'.

Stephan Roman tells us that Hugh was the first Westerner to meet the last surviving members of this community that had once numbered 50,000.

'He was fascinated by the extent to which they had preserved their customs and culture, their Hebrew language, and their separate identity, which dated back to the time of Nebuchadnezzar.'

Despite the political troubles and turmoil that had affected Yemen in the 1960's, Hugh noted that relations between Arabs and Jews in Sa'dah remained good and that the two communities got on well. No publicity was given to these findings, and when Hugh told the Yemeni Prime Minister of what he had discovered, the latter was completely astonished and took a considerable amount of persuading to believe the truth of what Hugh was telling him. Hugh's book *Seen in the Yemen* includes an account of the visit, and the original record is at Kew.

Two boys from the residual Jewish community in Sa'dah encountered by HRL.

A view of Sa'dah in Yemen where HRL located a Jewish community in 1971, a high point in his life and a great source of pride.

Thanos Petouris says: 'In the context of Yemen he was always very proud of his journey there…during which he came across the Jewish community of Sa'dah at a time that everyone thought that all Yemenite Jews had migrated to Israel.'

In October 1971 Hugh took leave and went to find the mystical Lake Shiwa, and the source of the Amu Darya, the river Oxus. He lectured the Royal Society for Asian Affairs on his discoveries in 1986, and in 1998 followed up with an expedition searching for the source of the other great historical river, the Syr Darya or Jaxartes. Both journeys appeared in articles he wrote for the Society's journal *Asian Affairs*.

LIFE UNDER THE PYRAMIDS

A Unique Household

In 1973, Hugh was posted as First Secretary to the Embassy in Cairo. Despite his reservations, his four years there probably proved to be the happiest time of his life. Much of this enjoyment stemmed from the location he chose for his home there – a great rambling house with twenty-one rooms, close to the Pyramids.

Typically, and in spite of its capacious size, as General Pascoe recalls, 'Hugh chose to sleep in a tent in his garden because he liked to hear the local sounds in the morning…whether of birds or the bugle calls from the nearby Egyptian Army barracks. It was here that he instructed his houseboy in various bugle calls which he had invented so that he could order drinks for his guests as they sat in the garden…Hugh sounded the calls for gin and tonic or whisky, followed by a number of Gs to indicate the number of drinks required.'

The Egyptians took Israel by surprise in 1973 by sending forces across the Suez Canal on 'Yom Kippur' to attack the Israeli forces who had been in occupation of Sinai since the Six-Day War in 1967. The Embassy had minimal, if any, forewarning of the attack. Hugh himself was on the point of travelling to stay with Willie Morris in Jeddah but cancelled the journey at the last minute. In general, he had close working relations with Egyptian contacts, regaling them with the memory that during his earlier service in southern Arabia, the radio station 'Voice of the South' – a propaganda outlet for Nasser's Egypt at the time – had reported his death three times. After the fighting of the Yom Kippur War had subsided, he took part in an official visit organised by Egyptian hosts to a location at the southern end of the Suez Canal where they had on display a group of fifteen Israeli tanks. These were originally Centurions that Britain had

Opposite: The view from Hugh's house towards the Pyramids with Subhi, Martha and the cat.

47

sold off after use. Hugh wondered if one of them had been his at Suez in 1956.

This brings us to Mohammed Aboudi, known to a succession of British officials in Cairo as 'Mo'. Mohammed Aboudi had begun his career as a house servant to Sir Miles Lampson, British High Commissioner to Egypt during the Second World War. When Hugh took up his posting to Cairo in 1972, a colleague in the Embassy urged him to rescue Mo from employment as under-cook of a junior member of the Spanish Embassy who 'did not know who Mo was'. Mo worked for Hugh for the four years he spent in Cairo. During that time, there were around three hundred visitors to Hugh's house beside the Pyramids. They came, Hugh would say, not to see him but to see Mo. Mo's life had been recorded in *Mo and other originals* by a previous British ambassador, Sir Charles Johnston (for whom Mo worked for twenty-six years). Hugh bought twenty-five copies and if any visitor stayed for a week, a copy signed by Mo was duly presented.

David Sands, Hugh's fellow officer in the Royal Tank Regiment, recalled 'Christmas with Mo': 'I looked at it; the children looked at it. I looked at it once more, picked up my spoon and led the charge. Mo stood beaming happily; he had broken us in. After a shaky start, we had eaten his acclaimed porridge.

'We had arrived the night before in response to Hugh's telegram: "This is your last chance to see Cairo as it should be seen. Come now for Xmas…"

'Hugh had failed to mention that, during our visit, the Christian Christmas and the Islamic equivalent would coincide for the first time in a thousand years. Cairo airport was bedlam. Bodies were strewn everywhere; some brewing coffee, some playing cards, some sleeping, some shouting amicably at each other, and inevitably most were arguing with officials of various types…

'We never truly appreciated our arrival at "Chez Hugh". Huge gates swung open as soon as our lights struck; servants appeared from every direction to lift out the children and carry them away or to take our baggage. Standing on the top step, leading into a striking three-storey house, was a majestic figure giving out

Mo, HRL's major domo, was a unique character, loved and admired by all who visited.

5 Sharia Yasmin, HRL's house in Cairo. Rosalind Wade Haddon describes this timber-framed building as 'charming but dilapidated'. 'Life,' she says, 'was never dull there'.

HRL, with Mohammed Aboudi (Mo) and other members of the eighteen-strong 'family' who lived in his garden.

orders, quietly but emphatically. This was Mo, major-domo to Hugh and clearly in command of the household. Somehow or other we were all shepherded into rooms, bathed, bedded and left to sleep.

'We eventually woke to a gentle tapping on the door. A beaming Mo appeared with a tray of tea and biscuits. As he drew the curtains, we heard squeals of delight from the children down the corridor. We looked out of the windows and saw the reason why. The house was on the threshold of the Pyramids of Giza. We felt that if we reached out, we could touch them. This scene heralded a kaleidoscope of events over the next ten days that not only captivated the children but delighted and enriched us all.'

David Sands' account goes on to describe a long day when Hugh took them on a camel trek to the Pyramids, 'a day which would be forever burnt into our memories...Mo directed his minions to pamper the adults with tea, sweetmeats and evil-smelling unguents; and summoned stilts and children from the resident families to occupy our children. As we all sank into this haven of pleasure and play, Mo excitedly told us of a change of plan. We were to go to the circus that evening...We didn't think there could be many surprises left but we were

wrong. We were to experience a seemingly endless series of special events, each heralded by Mo's dreadful porridge at breakfast; Mo's parrot, which reputedly was ninety years old, actually liked the stuff. But the bad porridge was compensated by Mo's beaming smile, genuine love of children, and total dedication to our well-being. And he worshipped Hugh.'

After four years with Hugh, Mo returned to Luxor, spending his last six months as a westernised personality, sitting on the bank of the Nile, where he was visited by passengers off tourist steamers. On his death in 1976, Hugh contributed an (anonymous)

Subhi, the junior assistant house-boy.

obituary to *The Times*, possibly the first time that a servant had an obituary in the newspaper.

A word must also be said about two other characters in Hugh's household. One of these was Subhi, a house-boy, probably no older than fifteen. His education had consisted only of a kindergarten stage, so Hugh took it on himself to teach Subhi to read and write in Arabic, setting him to work on exercises in copying out fables with titles such as 'Sulaiman and the Hoopoe' or 'The Lion and His Adviser, the Donkey'. A poem by the Egyptian writer Ahmad Shauki was also part of the 'curriculum'. Less formally, Hugh also taught Subhi and the gardener's daughter how to walk on stilts.

The other character was the resident parrot, Mr Pickwick, whom Hugh had 'inherited' from a colleague in Jeddah. Parrots have a reputation for picking up the most unlikely expressions and Mr Pickwick was no exception. On Fridays, people from the Embassy would bring their children out to the Pyramids for horse-riding and on an open invitation from Hugh, would drop in at his house. If he was absent, Mo and Subhi would offer coffee. Visitors also had scope to talk to the parrot. Hugh came home one day and found Mr Pickwick saying, 'Be a good boy, darling.' It became Hugh's habit every morning to repeat 'Good Morning, Mr Pickwick' in Arabic and also 'Be a good boy, darling', in English, to encourage the parrot to continue saying it.

The young Subhi, whose English was limited, heard those expressions every day and must have assumed that they were formal greetings. The upshot was that some months later, when the ambassador, Sir Philip Adams, and Lady Adams came for dinner, Mo and Subhi, spick and span in starched *gellabiyyah*, were ready at the door. Subhi, wanting to show off his English as the ambassador and his wife arrived, greeted them with 'Be a good boy, darling'.

This utterance by Subhi became the punchline of one of Hugh's favourite anecdotes. Apparently, it was also long remembered within the ambassador's family and at the funeral of a senior relative, one of the Adams grandchildren was heard to say, 'Be a good boy, darling', a kind of *envoie*!

Mr Pickwick himself lived on beyond the posting in Cairo and was taken to Sana'a in the YAR. From there, Hugh took him on to Khartoum. Six months after Hugh left at end-of-posting, the bird died. His body was bricked into a wall of the new embassy premises near a stone inscribed to read, 'In Memoriam. Mr Pickwick 1908–1984, a parrot with a distinguished record of public service'.

James Nash, who had looked after Mr P for a spell many years before, recalled: 'After a year Hugh moved to Riyadh and I took over his house, with his horse, several dogs and, temporarily, his parrot, Mr Pickwick. Sometime later, the parrot died and I received a disc, a brilliantly funny recorded funeral service for Mr Pickwick, and I could not resist a reply, in the form of an epitaph:

There was a parrot that I knew,

Ward of that famous Captain, Hugh,

A bird of elegance and note

That wore a fine grey morning coat.

An Orientalist, it swore

In Hindi, Arabic and more

Tongues that its mentor, Captain Hugh,

Could claim, in justice, that he knew,

But the bird has died, alas

And Hugh has sung its Avian Mass.

No '*Times*' obituary it had

Which is perhaps a little sad,

But as it would not be averse

To some memorial in verse,

This doleful tale I will relate

And be its parrot laureate.'

Captain Leopold Lazard
Diplomat and Ringmaster

In 1972, during an extended leave from his posting in Cairo, Hugh spotted an advertisement in *World's Fair*, a publication for circus and fairground people. It offered a half share in a circus run by 'Count' Andre and William Larzard. This struck a chord; he was predisposed in favour of circuses, not only from enjoyment of circus shows in boyhood, but also because, for him, the circus shared a discipline with military life. The logistics of putting up and taking down the big top and moving the troupe on to the next location demanded skills of exact and safe organisation.

Hugh saw a significance in the number of former army officers who featured in circus history. One such, Sergeant Major Astley of the 5th Light Dragoons, started the first circus in Britain in 1768 and had been rewarded with the gift of a white charger by King George III. In Hugh's own lifetime, former army captain Bertram Mills had run a popular circus. Hugh found himself missing the army and to some extent this added to his enthusiasm for the circus. He decided to appraise the show by joining it for a few days in Yorkshire...and bought that half share.

In consequence, the circus he part-owned, previously styled as the 'Circus Americano', went to Cairo for a month in 1973. There, under the description 'Circus Britannia', it performed jointly with the Egyptian State Circus.

Don Stacey points out that Hugh had his own visiting card printed, proclaiming him 'Captain Leopold Lazard'* and an Egyptian national newspaper published an article headlined, 'The British Lion is back in Egypt but in a circus cage'.

The British press got wind of a story and the *Daily Express* 'William Hickey' column ran an item entitled 'The British diplomat who wants to join a circus'. Hugh didn't suppose that the British Foreign Secretary was particularly amused by this adventure. Questions were asked in official telegrams from London. However, the Ambassador to Cairo at the time, Sir Philip Adams, staunchly defended the circus, declaring that it was 'the best thing that had happened to the British Embassy for some years'. Martin Burton (aka Zippo) echoes this: 'His Ambassador thought that Circus Britannia, which toured the Nile Valley, was

*Hugh adopted a simplified spelling of the Larzard name.

The lure of the circus. While on leave from Cairo, HRL was entranced by Circus Americano which he visited in Yorkshire.

HRL as Snoop Dog clown, Choumert Square, 2008. He would muse that his interest in the circus may have been via his maternal four times great-grandmother, Susanna Grimaldi. He was intrigued by the idea that she might have been related to the world-famous Joseph Grimaldi (1779-1837).

An unlikely scene for which HRL was entirely responsible. Nichola Larzard (sic) and Carlos Michelli from the Circus Britannia pose in an unfamiliar setting.

The Circus Britannia, an Anglo-Egyptian project, in which 'Princess Sakina' represents Britain for the exchange of flags. Inset: Calling card for HRL's alter ego Captain Leopold Lazard, Ringmaster for Circus Britannia in Egypt.

a welcome enhancement of the UK's cultural status.' Hugh himself believed that Egyptians were impressed that he, a 'stuffed-shirt diplomat' could spend his spare time as a ringmaster and that many new doors were opened to him as a result. The Circus Britannia did not last long after the death of 'Count Andre Maximillian Larzard' and Hugh's involvement (and finance) ended in 1974.

Hugh's connection with the circus world continued, however, and he later became an associate board member of Martin Burton's Academy of Circus Arts, whose aim was to teach people circus skills, the young especially.

Don Stacey reminds us that Hugh 'was a member of the Circus Friends Association of Great Britain…[and] also used to attend the circus day events in the Houses of Parliament staged by the Association of Circus Proprietors of GB'. He also wrote a monograph 'From Rome to Ringling: A World History of the Circus' and lectured on the subject to the English Speaking Union and others. But one thing he was adamant about: he would never give away any circus act secrets.

Hugh remained in contact with Carlos Michelli, a stilt walker who read *The Clown's Prayer* at Hugh's memorial service. Chris Barltrop, a leading figure in British circus for over forty years, said of Hugh: 'The circus world will be poorer without him.'

The Revd Bob Hicks was rector at Hinton St George. His memories of Hugh provide a delightful and appropriate footnote. Bob said: 'There is another image of Hugh that I personally will treasure all my days; it is after the Hinton village fête a couple of years ago. It was late in the afternoon, and Hugh was finally heading home. Dressed in shirt, jacket and tie. All but marching down Abbey Street in his jaunty but upright military manner. Hands behind his back. Proud, confident, relaxed. That was Hugh. And then I noticed that he had his face painted as a clown's. That was Hugh too.'

Hugh found it difficult to take farewell of his household 'family' when the time came to depart from Egypt en route for further responsibilities in Yemen. He had been in his entertaining element there. Friends well remember his panache and engaging sense of fun, and this in a war-time context, both before and after the Yom Kippur War of 1973. Egyptian regulations limited the scope for westerners to move around the country, but Hugh's ability to

Heading home...

Janette encounters snow on her journey to England after the completion of HRL's posting to Cairo.

speak fluent Arabic enabled him to strike up conversations wherever he went and stood him in good professional stead. His record of firm public service in Egypt contributed to his award of the OBE in 1977.

At the end of his posting in Egypt, Hugh drove back home in his Citroen, Janette, travelling with a friend, Theodora Mugnaini. They took a ferry from Alexandria to Venice and drove on through Italy and France, taking in a visit to the legendary explorer and author Dame Freya Stark in the Dolomites on their way home to England.

This visit was an impulsive affair *sans invitation* – Hugh had never met the eighty-two-year-old before – but, in his words, 'during a long afternoon and evening I found we shared many interests in common, among them a deep affection for the Arab world, the poetry of Matthew Arnold and 1930s screw-thread Leica cameras'.

It was the start of a long friendship. Twice she joined Hugh for extended stays in Sana'a, recorded in his book *Seen in the Yemen*. Over the next sixteen years, the pair met up several times in London, and kept up a lengthy correspondence until Stark's death at the age of one hundred in 1993.

FROM SANA'A TO SUDAN

'A Rather Wild Country'

The history of the internal affairs of the YAR in the mid-1970s is notoriously complicated, viz. the assassination of two successive presidents in 1977 and 1978. Another violent event took place early in 1977. Qadhi Abdullah Al-Hajjri, a former YAR prime minister, was shot and killed in London together with his wife and a member of the YAR Embassy to the UK. This led to intense work for the British Embassy in Sana'a, including Hugh who had to field and follow-up requests from the YAR authorities for information about the incident. Responsibility for the shootings remained unexplained at the time but, whatever its root causes, they added fuel to the reputation of YAR as a rather wild country.

Werner Daum, who was posted to Sana'a about the same time as Hugh, gives a vivid picture of him as a friend: 'We met in 1975 or '76, in Sana'a. Hugh and the Italian ambassador were the only diplomats interested in the grandeur of Yemen's three thousand years of civilisational history. We became friends.

'The most exciting event during our posting to Sana'a was the following: we decided to climb the not rarely snow-capped Jabal Nabi Shu'ayb, Arabia's highest mountain, 3,760 metres...Both of us had been thinking about it before, but such a thing needs a companion and

Opposite: A local tribesman with his rifle, on the 6,000 foot Jabal Rada, in the Yemen.
Right: Morning ablutions in the Sudan desert, 1979.

there we were, the two of us. The climb was rather demanding. The last two or three hundred metres to the summit were very steep, strewn with rocks and boulders. I felt exhausted, but Hugh continued (more often than not on his four feet, the same with me) with his slow and steady and methodical advance. He arrived on the top about 100 metres ahead of me...I was not pleased: after all, Hugh was eight or nine years older than me!

'In Sana'a, Hugh hosted Dame Freya Stark, and I was invited for dinner at his place. I am grateful to him for having met such an extraordinary person. Hugh spoke good, fluent Arabic. That allowed him to move lightly around the remotest places.'

Professor Daum adds: 'Hugh was extremely curious. He wanted to know things, to understand them fully. His keen intellect and his intimate knowledge of Arab mores, combined with accessibility and at-home feeling with the locals were the keys to this.'

Stark was not the only writing celebrity to visit YAR while Hugh was there. Wilfred Thesiger travelled within the country in Hugh's company, for example on the Tihama, or coastal plain, along the Red Sea's eastern shore in the YAR. Hugh

Travelling with HRL in the Tihama, Yemen in 1977, Wilfred Thesiger treats a young man who visits their campsite.

kept up a friendship with both writers afterwards. Hugh was one of a small group who gave Thesiger a ninety-first birthday lunch at the Travellers Club in London. After Thesiger's death, Hugh contributed to a book of tributes compiled by the club.

Guy Burn recalled being in Piccadilly one day and 'ran into Hugh coming out of Hatchards, both of us properly dressed, unknown now, in pin-striped suit, striped shirt, stiff collar, coke hat and umbrella. Without missing a beat, he asked if I had time for lunch at the Travellers,

As in Cairo, it was important to occupy a house that offered 'something special'. This illustration demonstrates its distinctive Yemeni architecture.

and I had lunch with him and a third, equally properly dressed, desert man, W. Thesiger, which utterly made my day, perhaps year.'

Hugh's vast correspondence included a veritable who's who of the Arab world, luminaries such as Dame Violet Dickson and Colonel Sir Hugh Boustead: both, like Hugh, holders of the RSAA's prestigious Lawrence of Arabia memorial medal.

Houses: The Dual Life Begins

In the early 1980s, Hugh's elder sister Christine and her husband 'T' (Terence J. L. Hutchins) moved from Nibley Green, Wotton-under-Edge, to a house at Madley on the River Wye in Herefordshire and, as previously, shared the accommodation with Hugh. Incidentally, Hugh reckoned that the fishing rights were probably worth more than the house. Hugh occupied a wing of the house, and did most of the renovation work in it himself.

In 1996, changing circumstances meant that the house at Madley was sold and Hugh had to find somewhere very quickly. He originally considered Sherborne but liked Hinton St George well enough to settle in there: the shop, the church, the tearoom were village assets. However, for him the house in Brettingham

Canon Bridge House, Madley, Herefordshire, until 1996 the house Hugh shared with his sister Christine. HRL had a wing to himself, which he used during leaves. Martha is seen parked, left.

Court was not cosy like Choumert Square. In the event, it actually suited him well: an excellent outlook over the main park, a garage with plenty of room for Edwina, Martha and his bikes; easy access for the Somerset Levels; a convenient station for travel to London; a large basement office and the use of his next-door-neighbour's cellar for an extension of his workshop. Moreover, he could shut the door and disappear off to London or further afield, knowing that his neighbours would keep an eye on No.14. It is ironic that in spite of his misgivings about the property, it was here that he was to spend his last days.

Helen Baker looked after Brettingham Court for Hugh for many years. She tells how Hugh would spend most of the summer in Hinton, and paints this picture: 'Going to his house was something I looked forward to, as his home was the polar opposite to my family home. I had two small children, a TV and enjoyed the modern way of living. [At Hugh's] Radio Four played in the background of this house, where the only TV was in the basement office covered with a cloth and was only switched on for rare occasions. The house was filled with Middle Eastern wonders (see Appendix C), a real Aladdin's Cave! and I just loved it...

'Hugh kept everything and never threw anything away, so a lot of things became victims of age, becoming worn out or had just seen better days. The biggest problem we shared together was the curse of the moths that ate everything, leaving holes and destruction in beautiful rugs and throws. We would spray, vacuum, and sometimes freeze items in the deep freeze, and on very rare occasions throw things away just to try and obliterate them.'

At an earlier stage of domestic transition Hugh put an advert in *The Lady* magazine: 'Retired former army officer seeks temporary accommodation'. He was amused to get three replies, not offering a house, but asking for his hand in marriage.

Brettingham Court with Edwina in the foreground. In true Arab fashion, the door to No.14 was always open.

Four Years in Khartoum

In 1978 Hugh was posted to the Sudan. By temperament, he preferred working abroad rather than in London, which offered him less variety and independence. Khartoum would not have been at the top of every senior official's list of postings but, for Hugh, the ways of Muslim societies – and perhaps their distance from London – had almost an inverse attraction. Unlike the YAR, Sudan had a history of British administration until it became independent, peacefully, in 1956 and, unlike Aden and southern Yemen, there had not been a period of violent turbulence before the British left. By the late 1970s, memories of British administration were bound to be wearing thin, but the Sudanese on the whole were open and friendly to British officials. Hugh's interest in the history and nature of Islam made him particularly suited to grasping the importance of a momentum in parts of Sudanese society for whom western and secular models for political change had little or no attraction. Political programmes that were presented as truly Muslim and national were gaining ground.

The implications of such movement towards pure or puritanical programmes and promises based on religion were inevitably difficult for Sudan. Much of the population in the south was not Muslim and the more Islamic that a central government in the north might become, the stronger the aspirations in the south would be for autonomy or separate independence. Sudan remained under the military/nationalist government of President Nimeiri for the duration of Hugh's posting, but his observations helped to increase an understanding of new directions in political thought in Sudan.

As before, those who encountered Hugh in person in Sudan came away with vivid memories. Bruce Duncan had repaired cars with Hugh back in his Catterick days: 'I next met up with Hugh in Khartoum in 1981. At the time, he was the First Secretary in the British Embassy and I was on a Loan Service posting with the British Army Advisory Team, Sudan. One day there was a knock at our front door. I was out at the time, so my wife, Toni, responded. She had never met Hugh but had heard a lot about him from me and we'd also exchanged Christmas cards over the years. Opening the door, she saw a tall man wearing a quaint pair of glasses and dressed in Arab robes and sandals. He was clutching a bottle of whisky! "You must be Hugh!" she exclaimed. And so, our friendship was renewed.

'In Khartoum he lived in a ramshackle Arab dwelling crammed full of curiosities, including a noisy one-eyed African Grey parrot [Mr Pickwick], an antique 'ear-trumpet' gramophone and an 1880 harmonium. He often invited us there as a family and our four children, ranging in age from four to nine years, loved exploring his Aladdin's Cave and listening to all his stories. Our eldest, Alex, was even allowed to play the harmonium.'

Douglas Johnson, an American specialist on Sudan, recalled the harmonium in a letter to Sir Willie Morris in 1982: 'I think he must carry all his possessions with him from post to post...Aside from his books (almost a whole shelf on T. E. Lawrence, the last ten years of Blackwood's Magazine, various home guides to a number of subjects, both practical and esoteric – astronomy, home plumbing, etc.) he had a small pedal organ with a sign announcing a £10 fine for anyone who touched it (I don't know if he's ever imposed the fine, the sign seemed to have come with the organ). Then there were souvenirs from other postings.

'Living out of the normal expatriate neighbourhood, he is also able to receive visitors who come around just for a chat, and both Sudanese and Brits seem to feel free to do so at any time.'

Typically, Hugh had found the house without assistance from the Embassy. Werner Daum enjoys recalling Hugh's account of when the head of administration visited him 'to ascertain that the rate was commensurate and within the British government guidelines. The man walked through the rooms, finding it on the whole a bit modest for a diplomat supposed to entertain important personalities. Nevertheless, he was pleased with the low rent.

'At last they came to the kitchen. In the (obviously quite deep) sink, two rats were performing some droll movements, mostly on their hind legs. The man was shocked but, wishing to keep his composure, said, "They are quite fat!"

In November 1981, a church service was held at HRL's 'farm' at Butri on the banks of the Nile to celebrate his twenty-five years between the Nile and the Euphrates.

"No wonder, the way I feed them!" Hugh replied.'

Hugh also rented a farm, Butri, on the Blue Nile some miles outside Khartoum. Bruce Duncan says that he 'often invited us to spend weekends with him there. Butri was a very basic abode and the loo was a hole in the ground surrounded by a *barasti* [palm frond] screen. Bats would fly in and out of the void whilst you were using the facility, which could be unnerving.

'When there, Hugh would sound Last Post and Reveille at the appropriate times, standing on the banks of the Nile wearing his Sudanese *aragi* – a loose white cotton smock over baggy white cotton three-quarter-length trousers –

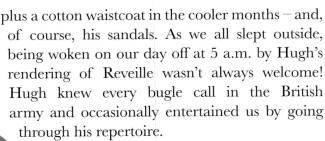

plus a cotton waistcoat in the cooler months – and, of course, his sandals. As we all slept outside, being woken on our day off at 5 a.m. by Hugh's rendering of Reveille wasn't always welcome! Hugh knew every bugle call in the British army and occasionally entertained us by going through his repertoire.

'On the Muslim (Thursday p.m./Friday) weekend 5th/6th November 1981, we were amongst a privileged group of friends invited down to Butri to celebrate the 25th anniversary of Hugh's service between the Nile and the Euphrates. We all slept out under the stars and next morning Hugh duly woke us up at dawn with Reveille. No lie in! Not even today!'*

Trevor Mostyn, too, vividly remembers lying under the stars after a nightcap of whisky, hearing the haunting sound of the bugle and seeing '…below us, where the Blue and White Niles met, the tall silhouette of Hugh playing the Last Post.'

Tom Walcot and his wife Judy stayed at Butri in 1987. They and Hugh were 'walking along the bank of an angry Nile when Hugh suggested that we should go in for a splash. So, we turned outwards, stripped off and then stepped into the water. Afterwards we faced outwards on the bank and dried off in the sun.'

In his presentations, for dramatic effect, Hugh would occasionally '…disappear and return wearing a *keffiyah*'.

*Bruce Duncan's book *The Loan Soldier* (Greenfinch Press) also included two references to Hugh.

Another member of the Embassy recalled how: 'Each Christmas we would set off to sing carols to the different foreign embassy residences, Hugh on the trumpet and me holding a broomstick with a lantern at the end. Hugh's lusty playing of "Hark the Herald Angels Sing" etc. completely and luckily drowned out my unmelodious singing.

'We were invited once into the East German residence; the Russians twitched their metaphorical curtains and the Chinese were silent. We ended up with the Americans who thought we were quite mad, but there we were refreshed with a large whisky or two!'

During his time in Khartoum, Hugh took leave to travel in Ladakh and Kashmir, but also explored more locally. In 1981 he wrote up – as he did with all his travels – a visit he made to Wau and Bahr Al Ghazal in an informal record that he titled 'Rural Rides in the Sudan'.

Hugh returned to Britain and, between 1982 and 1984, served on the Middle East desk where he was never '…suited to London office life and got very bored. He was once drafted into a section dealing with China to "broaden his experience" but Personnel very soon realised their mistake! When bored or tired he would lie fully dressed at full length on his desk and go to sleep, a sight the secretaries never quite got used to.'

During his final years of service, Hugh was called on to contribute to efforts to deepen understanding of trends in the Muslim Arab world. It was proving difficult to understand what might be described as 'radicalisation' in younger generations. He undertook an extensive study and duly presented his observations to a wide range of colleagues and other departments in UK both in writing and via presentations, where he frequently drew on his years in the Arab world to dramatise and enliven his lectures.

He could put alarming developments in a wider context and also offer explanations why extreme activists might perpetrate with a clear conscience actions that others found repellent. His knowledge was based on wide and meticulous reading, but he was no dry theorist. He was much in demand to give briefings, which were never dull. One of his subordinates described Hugh in full and lively flow as 'mesmeric'. Indeed, perhaps his ability to engage the interest of others in the Arab world was his most important legacy.

He retired on the day and at the hour he wanted: thirty-six years from when he had first joined the army: 23 June 1989.

Retirement
A Technical Term

A Constantly Open Door

'Retirement' was only a technical term in Hugh's case. A time of indolent leisure it most certainly was not. After over thirty years of public service, there followed a further twenty-five when Hugh engaged in many of the passions that had sustained him but he had not always been able to fully enjoy. Then, of course, there was the research and writing of his two books.

Paramount among his passions were his friends, of which he had very many and in whom he delighted. Both Choumert Square and Brettingham Court had a constantly open door into hospitality, companionship, story-telling and scholarship.

Hugh's daily relationship with the outside world matched his quaint unorthodoxy in other respects. He did not take a daily newspaper, only reading one when he picked one up on the train. If there was something in which he was interested, he might go and buy a copy. (Incidentally, being an inveterate conversationalist, he often picked up new friends on trains, too.) Not having a regular paper did not stop him writing to them: *inter alia* he had five letters published in *The Times* and two in the *Daily Telegraph*. And he somehow managed to accumulate articles from a wide range of publications, which he would copy many times and circulate to his friends. As for telephones, he did buy a mobile phone but claimed he had only ever got it to work once!

Choumert Square had no television, and Hugh rarely watched the one in Somerset although, as Rebecca Wilmshurst has alluded to, he did have a large collection of films on cassette. He frequently listened to the World Service on the wireless, rather than Radio 4. Latterly, he invested in a digital radio.

Opposite: Wearing a favoured *topi* from Himachal Pradesh.

HUGH AND FOOD

Keith Hamilton and Graham Reuby have many happy memories of shared outings and meals enjoyed together with Hugh: 'Hugh was always an extreme purist about his food and couldn't bear sauces, dressings or even seasonings of any kind – although, having said that, he was able to get over those scruples when it meant not having to cook for himself!' Ever conscious of his health and diet, he claimed to eat twelve to fourteen pieces of fruit each day. His early morning routine included five cups of tea before break-

fast. He was proud to still be able to get into an old suit made for him at Sandhurst.

HRL and his neighbour Averil Hughes are joined for lunch by a family from Kyrgyzstan.

Above all, considering how much he wrote, computer was there none. Tim Myatt quotes Hugh in a *Peckham Peculiar* article of 2014: '...I'll be going to the grave in not very long, and I hope I never know the difference between a computer and a commuter, a blog and a frog, an iPod and a tripod, a Blackberry and a gooseberry, and a Kindle and a spindle.'

He didn't even type, prevailing upon loyal friends to help. However, this didn't impede a vast and varied correspondence, even with those he saw on a regular basis, which kept the postmen busy in both London and Somerset. He assiduously replied to any letters he received, and never let drop his written Arabic. His Eid and Christmas card list was, not unsurprisingly, extensive.

Where to begin with Hugh's interests? Perhaps the most overriding joy of his life was literature: books and poetry...or was that equal to his love of motor cars and bikes? But then there was the circus. And music. And carpentry. And astronomy. And all this is to ignore the time Hugh spent on further travels and expeditions, the latter leading groups of younger people so that he could pass on his knowledge and spirit of adventure.

Hugh and Literature

In Choumert Square every spare wall had a bookcase and, between there and Brettingham Court, his library totalled nearly three thousand books. A large majority contained either a letter from the author, an obituary or some other relevant paper on the subject of the book which frequently linked Hugh directly with the author.

From school days he had loved poetry, with Matthew Arnold being his all-time favourite. Stephan Roman points out that Hugh considered *The Scholar-Gipsy* redolent of his childhood, Arnold's lines reflecting his own cycling round the same lanes from Abingdon to Bablock Hythe.

HRL captured reading on board the Clare College, Cambridge punt by a friend, Jane Tippett.

Hugh was not diffident about impromptu poetry recitals. Fellow travellers will recall the occasions when Arnold's tragic poem *Sohrab and Rustum* was quoted to unsuspecting local villagers in all manner of countries across Asia.

Stephan Roman also remembers his last cycle ride with Hugh, following the route of Robert Browning's famous *How They Brought the Good News from Ghent to Aix*. At the end of each daily ride, Hugh 'would regale the startled passers-by with public readings from the poem. His final recitation outside the cathedral in Aachen attracted a bemused, but wonderfully enthusiastic, crowd of over fifty people.' Hugh was a regular contributor to the Radio 4 programme 'Poetry Please' and laminated pages of poetry were among his papers: poems such as Auden's *Night Mail* and Arthur Clough's *Say Not the Struggle Nought Availeth*, and many others.

As his nephew Paul Swift touched on in his eulogy, Hugh was a great fan of George Borrow's novel *Lavengro* with its peripatetic protagonist – the 19th-century literary equivalent of a road movie. Hugh's passion for Borrow took him on pilgrimages to the poet's birthplace at East Dereham, Norfolk and, in Edwina, to public houses bearing his name in mid-Wales.

Steve Wilson offers a postscript to this: 'I was fortunate to meet Hugh Leach in the course of my work as a motoring journalist. He was initially courteous but a little distant. While he was fetching some maps of Central Asia, where

The Scholar-Gipsy

Go, for they call you, shepherd, from the hill;
Go, shepherd, and untie the wattled cotes!
No longer leave thy wistful flock unfed,
Nor let thy bawling fellows rack their throats,
Nor the cropp'd herbage shoot another head.
But when the fields are still,
And the tired men and dogs all gone to rest,
And only the white sheep are sometimes seen
Cross and recross the strips of moon-blanch'd green,
Come, shepherd, and again begin the quest!

Here, where the reaper was at work of late—
In this high field's dark corner, where he leaves
His coat, his basket, and his earthen cruse,
And in the sun all morning binds the sheaves,
Then here, at noon, comes back his stores to use—
Here will I sit and wait,
While to my ear from uplands far away
The bleating of the folded flocks is borne,
With distant cries of reapers in the corn—
All the live murmur of a summer's day.

Screen'd is this nook o'er the high, half-reap'd field,
And here till sun-down, shepherd! will I be.
Through the thick corn the scarlet poppies peep,
And round green roots and yellowing stalks I see
Pale pink convolvulus in tendrils creep;
And air-swept lindens yield
Their scent, and rustle down their perfumed showers
Of bloom on the bent grass where I am laid,
And bower me from the August sun with shade;
And the eye travels down to Oxford's towers.

Matthew Arnold

A familiar sight on the Somerset Levels. In August 2002, HRL cycled to Isle Brewers, the retirement parish of Reverend Dr Joseph Wolff, one of the many historical characters he researched and on whom he lectured.

Martha had travelled, as a writer, naturally I began to peruse his wonderfully eclectic bookshelves. When he returned, I made some remark about his copy of George Borrow's *The Romany Rye* [the sequel to *Lavengro*]. Hugh was immediately transformed, thunderstruck that a "muttering correspondent" should be familiar with a 19th-century author and kindred spirit.'

He had a fascination for the novel *Ali and Nino* by Kurban Said, set in Baku about a romance between a Muslim Azerbaijani boy and a Christian girl from Georgia. Hugh did considerable research into the origins of the story.

Dr Bijan Omrani found Hugh a great inspiration when he was starting work on his book *Afghanistan: A Companion and Guide* (Odyssey 2005). Bijan says: 'I first met him at Choumert Square in about 2003 and have very fond memories of enthralling conversations sitting amongst his remarkable collection of travel books. He was hugely generous with his time, assisting me with ideas and information about Afghanistan, Central Asia and his knowledge of Islam. He was an inspiration in that he was one of the last representatives of a great tradition of exploration – self-taught, hugely learned but not academic, conscious of the importance of the knowledge he had [gained] by travel, but never without a sense of the subversive and mischievous...'

'There's a Wind on the Heath Brother': Vagabonding with George Borrow

The itinerant life, writing and times of the celebrated mid-nineteenth-century author

The following is the introduction to a paper Hugh presented to the '63' Club, London, in 1997: 'They say one definition of retirement is that you have time to look at every volume in a second-hand book shop. But it was many years before my own retirement when I stopped to glance through a cardboard box of books outside such a shop in a back street of London, all marked at five shillings each. I was about to move on believing it contained the usual unsaleable collection of works on religion, mathematics and Latin Primers, when one title caught my eye – *Lavengro* by George Borrow. What a strange title, I thought. Its pages were interspersed by some fine pen and ink sketches of wild-looking men in outlandish garb standing in, or striding through, desolate landscapes. A gust of fresh air seemed to blow out from the pages.

'That night in bed I examined my purchase. I was transfixed. The strange archaic language of its text had both a calming and a disturbing effect on me. Calming, because of the soft precise Englishness of the narrative. But disturbing, and why that was I couldn't immediately fathom. It seemed to trigger off something inside me which I felt was best left untriggered. I was drawn to a childhood dream where I roamed open spaces with gypsy folk or toured the villages of central England with a small tenting circus. True, I later put some of these dreams into reality but at that time I had not. And who, I wondered, was this man who had re-awoken this atavistic urge.'

Unsurprisingly, Hugh took a great interest in the life of T. E. Lawrence. Richard Fell reports that 'his views on "new" books on Lawrence were usually scathing.'

Hugh left his literary books to Abingdon School, and his Arabia and Asian titles to RSAA. These latter books are now lodged at Haileybury College as a separate collection to be known as the RSAA Hugh Leach Library at Haileybury. He had already given over twenty circus books to the University in Sheffield, which has the biggest collection of such literature.

Before we leave the subject, one endearing fact is that, despite his literary erudition, Hugh liked to read a chapter of one of his *Just William* books every night before he went to sleep!

Hugh and 'Things Mechanical'

Hugh carried out all the maintenance on his cars, motorbikes and bicycles himself, with a knowledge acquired over many years of a lifelong passion.

Adrian Steger writes: 'Then there were things mechanical. Cars: the Land Rover, the Humber and at one time a Citroen and a Vincent motorcycle. These and Leica Ill cameras were mechanisms he understood and could work with. A page of *The Times* could be used to set the gap in the points of a distributor cap and the sole of a shoe used to replace a big end gasket. He mastered what technology he wanted to...It was paradoxical that he relished getting news of the North-West Frontier from young Pakistanis with mobile phones in the market near Choumert Square...'

Always a keen carpenter, he had a workshop in both his London and Somerset houses, with numerous tools and bits and pieces that 'could be useful one day'. Around his house were a number of lamp bases and wooden boxes which he had made at school and, of course, the bookcases which he had built in both houses. Amongst Hugh's most valued possessions were a 1920s crystal set and an 1880s microscope and not to

Always keen on working with his hands, there were no less than five areas in his two houses where he kept tools, and items which 'could be useful one day'.

The early Leica lens-carrying case and some of the rare items it contained.

be forgotten were his two treasured Leica cameras, with an original leather case containing many lenses and other accessories – inevitably, another of his many skills was the ability to process his own photographs.

Hugh and Faith

Religion and faith meant a great deal to Hugh. His father's ecumenism rubbed off on him and, although baptised and confirmed in the Church of England, he was fascinated by the history and creeds of other faiths. For Hugh, all faiths were equally valid. He kept a Qur'an always open in his sitting room and was delighted when he was able to welcome Aramaic speakers to Brettingham Court, asking him for a loaf of bread in the words that Jesus would have used. He was not keen on missionaries who might try to convert people from their faith. [He was always careful not to eat in front of colleagues during Ramadan, and never ate in public if they were observing the fast.]

Stephan Roman writes: 'Hugh's deep knowledge and insights into different Muslim traditions earned him huge respect and admiration both in the UK and also internationally.'

'This strong interest in Islam was balanced by an equal fascination with early Christianity...He read widely on the subject and at one point declared himself to be a Nestorian Christian much to the bewilderment of a couple of Mormon missionaries who had turned up on his doorstep, hoping to convert him. Hugh was

Hugh's copy of the Qur'an was beside his bed when he died. On return to Brettingham Court, it fell open at Sura VI, a passage from which was included in his memorial service.

a great supporter of the Eastern Christians, particularly the Assyrian Church, and was very concerned by the impact of the Iraq War on Christians across the Middle East.'

Bijan Omrani says: 'One thing I greatly appreciated was that there was also a great sense – although treated lightly – of the spiritual, which he understood and drew from in the realm of the traveller and exploration. It came through as a golden thread in his eclectic obsessions such as with circus performers and also George Borrow – indeed, thanks to Hugh that great line of Borrow "There's a wind on the heath, brother" became a catchphrase amongst many of my friends.'

In 2005, Hugh invited his rector, Bob Hicks, to an RSAA lecture. This led to his being asked to do a short sermon on the plight of the Christian communities in Iraq. And so began the annual Remembrance Day sermons at Hinton St George, with subjects such as 'War Poetry', 'God and the Gun', 'The Role of the Padre in War' and 'Christianity in Iraq from the 1st century to today'. All revealed immense scholarship (see Appendix D). Bob said that it took him quite a while to get used to preaching when Hugh was in the congregation. 'He would always wear a deep frown right the way through the sermon, quite off-putting, until I realised that he was simply thoroughly engaged and thinking deeply about everything he was hearing. So actually a great compliment – and he always had a question for us to get stuck into afterwards.'

Hugh's faith manifested itself in many ways, not least in the encouragement he gave to youngsters, especially his ten godchildren. Very much shaped by his motherless childhood, Hugh would say that raising tribes was normal for him, whereas raising children was a real role. Three parents describe how Hugh took his responsibilities.

Diana Berridge: '[Hugh]was a kind and generous godfather, and the source of some unusual gifts...Jonathan received four pounds of dates for his first birthday in 1968!...Then there was the Circus Americano, of which Hugh was a co-director. Written on the flyleaf of *The Circus Boy* by Ruth Manning-Saunders was, "The bearer of this book is my godson. Please may he be admitted to a ringside seat."'

Bob Pascoe: 'He was godfather to one of my daughters and never missed her birthday. His presents were always different and interesting. One year she received three little parcels of different coloured silk. Inside one was a small piece of frankincense, a second had a piece of myrrh while the third contained a small gold charm.'

David Sands: 'He was godfather to my eldest son. Like most bachelors, he was a conscientious one. Someone who wrote him letters on bark stripped from the paper tree on the snow-line in the Afghanistan mountains... Someone who rode for seven days on a camel to cut a section of the Hejaz Railway, marked 1917; not a railway set as first thought, but now a doorstop... Someone who never forgot no matter where he was or what he was doing.'

Other young people, although not godchildren, were greatly influenced by Hugh and valued the interest and encouragement he gave them. Alexander Evans paid this tribute: 'Hugh was a fine man, and personally very kind to me over the years...His excitement for Asia – and for public service – helped inspire mine.'

Charles Timmis adds: 'I first met Hugh at the age of four years, clinging for dear life as pillion on his Vincent motorbike when he visited my parents (my father being a lifelong army friend). Hugh was a huge influence – as an example, friend, mentor and guide – always having time for you, nurturing ideas and inspiring adventures. I would always hugely value the visits and discussions at Choumert Square and Brettingham Court, poring over books and maps, meeting other interesting people, and always leaving with more ideas and inspiration. This led, for me, to a great love of Asia and, in particular, Pakistan, its mountains, people, history and character. Hugh still inspires the paths I take.'

Deborah Cassidi put together an anthology *Favourite Prayers: chosen by people from all walks of life*. Hugh contributed two items, which speak of the man and his faith. The first was *Be Strong* by Maltbie D. Babcock (1858–1901).

Be Strong!

We are not here to play, to dream, to drift;
We have hard work to do and loads to lift;
Shun not the struggle, face it, 'tis God's gift.
Be strong, be strong, be strong!
Be strong!
Say not the days are evil—who's to blame?
And fold the hands and acquiesce—O shame!
Stand up, speak out, and bravely, in God's Name.
Be strong, be strong, be strong!
Be strong!
It matters not how deep entrenched the wrong,
How hard the battle goes, the day, how long;
Faint not, fight on! Tomorrow comes the song.
Be strong, be strong, be strong!

Hugh's second entry was *The Schoolboy's Prayer*: 'Vouchsafe, O Lord, that I get through this day without being found out.' Another of Hugh's treasured verses was from *Poems from the Desert* by Lieutenant P. W. R. Russell:

'Thanks be to you that I can still
Enjoy, O God, your wonders – still can thrill
Each sunrise and each sunset at the sight
Of flaming red that puts the clouds to flight: …
O God – it's great to be alive.'

Hugh very much admired something that Graham Greene had said: 'the older I get, the greater becomes my doubt, but the stronger becomes my belief'. Indeed, Hugh told friends he reckoned this 'the wisest thing ever said'.

If evidence is needed of Hugh's approach to his non-spiritual life, then an answer may lie in the Arabic on his bookplate (p. viii), alternatively translated as 'The disasters of life are not to be laughed at' or 'The disasters of life are there to be laughed at'. Hugh preferred the second option.

Hugh's Scholarship

Hugh's immense scholarship shone out whenever he set pen to paper. This is just one remarkable example, part of a Christmas letter Norman Cameron received from him in 2012:

'You ask about the early 2nd century onwards Christian heretics. Alas, my notes, if I haven't destroyed them, are all in Somerset. But speaking from memory there were heretical movements such as the Ebionites (1st–2nd), Badaisans (2nd–3rd), Docetists, Donatists, Manicheans, Marcians, Montanists, Sabellians etc. Re: Najran (then Yemen, now Saudi Arabia), yes Yemen was then under Jewish rule. This after the elite Himyaritic community converted to Judaism in the 4th century and the Himyaritic King Yusuf Asar, also known as Dhu Nuwas, declared war on the Christian Ethiopians in Yemen and ordered the massacre of the Najran community...'

Hugh as Author

Hugh was asked by the Council of the Royal Society for Asian Affairs to write a history of the Society to commemorate their centenary. The result was *Strolling About on the Roof of the World – The First Hundred Years of the Royal Society for Asian Affairs* published in 2003 by RoutlegeCurzon.

Susan Maria Farrington worked with Hugh on his books and describes what went into this one: 'In preparing to write the book, Hugh would spend long

At work on *Strolling About on the Roof of the World*.

hours in the Society's archives, reading every journal and minute, eventually amassing a long run of ring-binder folders containing copies of material. The first draft was written entirely in pencil, on lined foolscap paper. Drafting appeared to come effortlessly to him and he had great skill in telling a complex story in a straightforward manner.' He persuaded Sue to help with the typing, but additionally she took on research and photography. 'Hugh's attention to detail was phenomenal,' Sue continues, recalling the many occasions when 'he would telephone with a minor correction to "line six, para three on page such-and-such". The typescript would be duly amended but Hugh would then add "while you have the machine on, please go on two more pages…" After other changes and even complete paragraph re-drafts over the telephone, it was not uncommon for me to have to say "Hugh, it's 2.45 a.m. and I think I need to get to bed".'

Based on his travels with Dame Freya Stark in the 1970s, Hugh's second book *Seen in the Yemen* echoes Freya's *Seen in the Hadhramaut* published in 1938 by John Murray. As early as 1977, Freya and Hugh had been in touch with John Murray with a view to such a publication, but it was not until 2011 that it saw the light of day. Hugh took immense care with the selection of the photographs, and such details as the layout, colour of the paper etc.

Rosalind Wade Haddon was working on a photographic project for the National Museum in Sana'a at the time and recalls that 'the autumn of 1977 was a period of uncertainty in Yemen's turbulent history following the assassination of the president of what was then North Yemen. Hugh was working on the idea of *Seen in the Yemen* and spent a lot of time going round the old city capturing scenes that we knew were fast disappearing. He had a fully equipped darkroom in his house where we developed and printed the black and white film immediately after these outings.'

With Freya Stark in the mountains of the Yemen. She shared with him a passion for black and white photography using their 1930s Series III screw-thread Leicas.

John Harding writes: 'For all his many achievements, Hugh's most lasting monument may be his book *Seen in the Yemen*...This beautiful work reveals Hugh's innate artistic talents and combines an outstanding collection of sepia photographs with a scholarly text and an account of his 1971 rediscovery of the Yemen's last remaining Jewish community.'

These are acknowledged in the accompanying note to his contributions to *Envoys to the Arab World, Vol. II, The MECAS Memoirs 1944–2009*: 'His extensive memoirs lodged in the MECAS archive, together with splendid black and white photographs and maps, record his many long journeys of exploration in the remoter parts of Arabia.'

عيد ميلاد سعيد

كل عام و أنتم بآلاف خير

كل عام و بلا بل تغني سيدة سلامكم سيناتيك

Happy BirThday

Many Happy and Healthy returns

May the nightingales sing in the peace of your garden forever.

Every happy wish and many million thanks for all your help and Support.

With lots of love from

Hugh

82

The stylistic quality of Hugh's writing was equal to his scholarship and his dedication. Jenny Harding-Rolls says: '…He wrote such wonderful letters, always including a perfect Arabic quote in immaculate handwriting, to be treasured always…'

As to the mechanics of his writing, Norman Cameron, in reflecting on Hugh's life, commented that 'it seems slightly disloyal to Hugh to offer these memories in Word-document form, since he himself always wrote with eloquent ease in pen and ink. [Hugh was left-handed; his writing small and very distinctive]. He lived a total non-screen life but he was not a destructive Luddite. He recognised, for example, that his beloved Land Rover and his sit-up-and-beg bicycles belonged to a passing era. What he did challenge, however, was a narrow-minded insistence that modernity was necessarily better than before. For him, the process of transferring thought to page was more immediate via the pen.'

Hugh's riveting effect on audiences has been mentioned and his diaries reveal a constant programme of lectures on many topics to a variety of organisations: the Joint Services Command and Staff College; his old school, Abingdon; RSAA; day seminars at Dillington House, Somerset; English Speaking Union; South Somerset Peace Group; Ebenezer Presents on the Somerset Levels; Hinton St George village hall, etc. etc. In Somerset, these were almost invariably reported in the local papers, frequently with illustrations.

Occasionally he would enlist the help of 'visitors' to enhance his presentations. Steve Wilson attended a lecture he gave at Abingdon School on current Middle Eastern affairs: 'He enlivened this by excusing himself from the stage and returning, first as a bearded Islamist, and then, in a *burqah*, as the latter's female counterpart.' All this in addition to the Remembrance Day sermons at Hinton St George already mentioned.

In commenting on the many articles, reviews and talks that Hugh wrote, Adrian Steger says: 'Each one was meticulously researched and prepared. "An hour's work for a minute's talk", he would say.'

Hugh served as member of the RSAA's Council, was the recipient of one of its distinguished awards, became an Honorary Vice-President and, after the death of long-serving secretary Marinel FitzSimons, its Historian. He rightly described himself as 'the necessary elephant's memory of the Society.' Hugh's vast knowledge and network of friends led to his frequently being asked to write obituaries, including one as his contribution to the Society's tribute to Sir Wilfred Thesiger (see Appendix E).

Hugh and the RSAA

Hugh was dedicated to the RSAA and could always be relied on to be present at Society events. He was warmly remembered by many RSAA members:

'He was the inspiration for my joining the RSAA and we shall miss him.'
Eliza, Lady Conyngham

'He was a man of such erudition and knowledge, as well as being lovely to talk to.'
David Tomlinson

'He would not mind leaving behind a reputation for slightly barmy fun. He cultivated it after all and liked the centre-stage.' Norman Cameron

'He was a delightful man, we had "adventure travel" in common, and I am sure he will be very much missed by his friends and the RSAA'. John Hare

Rebecca Wilmshurst says, 'To quote Ophelia out of context, when she spoke of Hamlet's "noble mind… the courtier's, soldier's, scholar's, eye, tongue, sword" she might, had she known him, have been thinking of Hugh Leach.

'The very mention of Hugh's name stirs very particular thoughts: of the explorer, the multi-culturalist, the historian, the scholar who understood the origins of Christianity and the complexities of Islam, the educator who generously shared his knowledge through lectures, books and pamphlets that were impeccably researched, rehearsed, informed and entertaining. Many will have tales to tell of his derring-do in conflict and in the fields of international and domestic diplomacy.'

Hugh's generosity is reflected in a charming reminiscence from Bill Colegrave: 'I was giving a lecture at RSAA on the Wakhan Corridor and the source of the Oxus (following publication of my book *Halfway House to Heaven*)…The day before the lecture I had a call from RSAA asking me if I knew Hugh. I said that I did not but explained that there could be confusion about the minutiae of our respective claims, given that he had lectured to the Society on "A Ride to Shiwa: A Source of the Oxus".

'They said that I should be warned that it was Leach who would deliver the thanks/review of my lecture the next day, and that Leach considered the Oxus and the Wakhan to be very much his parish, and his alone, within RSAA and generally. I did at least take the precaution of mentioning his work in suitably complimentary terms in my lecture. At the end of my talk, a tall man arose in the audience. As he did so, he said, for all to hear; "I am sorry to say that Mr Colegrave has made one very serious error today". I knew at once that this was Hugh Leach.

Sunset over the Oxus.

'Silence followed as he made his way to the front...and I was expecting the worst review. As he arrived, he continued: "...and that is to acknowledge me as a greater expert than he himself on the Wakhan".'

The year after his death, RSAA established the 'Hugh Leach Memorial Lecture'. As the citation in *Asian Affairs* states, it should be delivered 'by a noted scholar and/or traveller/explorer to cover any or preferably a combination of the following subjects reflecting Hugh's interest in the Middle East and Central Asia – exploration, recent history and military history, travel, eccentric travellers, history of Islam etc.' It should also 'be given in the spirit of Hugh Leach – combining deep scholarship and experience with the lightness, eccentricity and joy which were the keynotes of his character.'

To date, the prestigious lecturers have been:

2016 - 'Suez at Sixty'. James Barr
2017 - 'From the "Old Turkey" to the "New Turkey": How did it happen and how much does it matter?'. Mr David Barchard
2018 - 'Partition: The Story of Indian Independence and the Creation of Pakistan in 1947'. Lt General Sir Barney White-Spunner KCB CBE
2019 - 'The Genealogy of Terror: How to distinguish between Islam, Islamism and Islamist Extremism'. Dr Matthew L. N. Wilkinson
2020 - 'Political Quietism in Islamic Societies: A Neglected Tradition'. Dr Saud Al-Sarhan
2021 - 'The Afghanistan File: Saudi Arabia and Afghanistan'. His Royal Highness Prince Turki Alfaisal bin Abdulaziz Al Saud

Travels and Expeditions

An Inspiration to Many

Britain has a centuries-long history of sending expeditions to the East and the RSAA's 'tours' for members – which Hugh had joined – had played a recent part in this history. However, it was Hugh who suggested a new possibility: that the Society might revive an idea dating back to 1922, by sponsoring a Young Persons' Expedition to the Western Himalayas, introducing them to the joys of high-altitude trekking. The idea was approved.

As might be expected, Hugh's preparation was thorough, and he sought the advice of the best brains. Amongst these was Brigadier Jan Nadir Khan, the founder of Adventure Foundation Pakistan (AFP). AFP was, and is, a non-profit organisation giving young Pakistanis an opportunity to participate in adventure activities in their own country in an 'Outward Bound' concept. Hugh felt he was in such safe hands with Brigadier Jan that the Pakistan expeditions were conducted under the aegis of the AFP. Hugh was further delighted to become AFP's honorary representative in UK.

Hugh also asked Jon Fleming of the British Schools Exploring Society at the Royal Geographical Society for advice. The question: 'As a matter of interest, what happens if you have a mixed expedition?' The answer: 'You must have three-person tents: two girls and one boy, or one girl and two boys as it is not a "spectator sport".'

Adrian Steger documents that Hugh was to go on 'many expeditions and explorations in the ranges of the western Himalayas. Others were to a source of the Oxus and Kyrgyzstan. Many were with youngsters.'

In July 1992, shortly before departure for Pakistan, the first expedition trained in

Opposite: On a recce of the Naltar valley and Phakora Pass in northern Pakistan, July 1992.

With Brigadier Jan Nadir Khan, President of
Adventure Foundation Pakistan, after the first of four
RSAA Young Persons' expeditions in Pakistan, 1992.

the Black Mountains, Wales. (Although in his late fifties, Hugh reckoned he was much fitter than the boys). Then came the expedition. Chris Hawley says: 'The trip was a truly memorable and character-building experience in which we were pushed to physical and mental limits over a period of three weeks. However, my lasting memory will be of the daily Reveille which we were subjected to by Hugh's bugle, forcing us out of bed and pushing us on to the day ahead!'

Adrian Mutton adds an amusing 'Hugh' postscript: 'As a seventeen-year-old, sitting in a packed auditorium in early 1992 at Abingdon School, I listened to Hugh Leach tell of tales of the East. His talk was full of history, adventure and intrigue. Hugh was offering to take one lucky member of the audience to the Karakorams on the Society's first Young Persons' Expedition, which he and Adrian Steger went on to lead that summer. I applied and still to this day only believe I got a place on the tour because I told Hugh in my interview that I could play the bugle and he was delighted to have someone on the expedition who could sound Reveille (as it happened [Christopher Hawley] was a far better player than I and even he was usually beaten to the camp fire in the morning by Hugh who would already be on his third cup of tea by sunrise).

'The trip to Pakistan shaped the rest of my life. Enthralled by the adventure (and as Adrian Steger will tell you it was quite an adventure!) after returning from the expedition I formed part of the Society's first Young Persons Committee and immediately I applied for any gap-year job I could find in South Asia. I was invited to teach English and Economics in Saharanpur, a third-tier city in Uttar Pradesh. Without the benefit of the internet then, I relied on Hugh doing some research for me in the Society's library. He sent me a rather glowing report which read: "Adrian, Saharanpur sounds like a gem of a city. It is at the foothills of the Himalayas with a river flowing through it, has a wonderful botanical garden, a famous wood market and the most delicious mangoes in India"...Within a few weeks I was on a plane to India. I arrived in Saharanpur to find that the Himalayas had moved 500 miles, the river was a toxic cesspit, the botanical gardens had overgrown and had been padlocked since the 1960s, the wood market was still active but a degraded shambles...The mangoes, however, were indeed delicious. I wrote to Hugh from my mosquito-ridden school digs (I soon caught malaria) and asked him where he got his information from, and to update him on the current state of the city. His response was that he had found various records from between the mid-19th and early 20th centuries!'

In addition to the five Young Persons' Expeditions, (four in Pakistan and one in India) Hugh was to join three RSAA Tours (1990, 1991 and 1994), and, in 1998, journeyed in search of the sources of the Jaxartes (Syr Darya) in Kyrgyzstan with Adrian Steger, Isobel Shaw and Sue Farrington, following up on his 1971 Oxus expedition.

A particular high spot was the 1994 expedition, which took the title 'Racing Kelly Across the Roof of the World' commemorating the legendary Chitral Expedition. (To relieve besieged forces there in late winter 1895, Colonel James

YOUNG PERSONS' EXPEDITIONS

1992: Pakistan (RSAA) *From the Himalayas to the Hindu Raj*

1994: Pakistan (Abingdon School) *Racing Kelly across the Roof of the World*

1995: India (RSAA) *Young Persons' Expedition to Northern India*

1996: Pakistan (Culford School) *Hindu Kush Expedition*

1997: Pakistan (Royal Russell School CCF) *To the Edge of the Wakhan and Back*

During the 1997 Royal Russell School CCF expedition in the Hindu Kush, northern Pakistan, the group descend to their camp at Chikar after an acclimatisation exercise before tackling the 15,000 foot Darkot Pass.

Encouraging a member of the 1994 Abingdon School expedition across a mountain stream during their trek from Gilgit across three mountain passes westwards to Chitral.

Kelly, and more than a thousand men, had 'impossibly' trekked with field guns one hundred and fifty miles over the mountains from Gilgit to Chitral).

Hugh had high praise for the students from his old school, Abingdon; nevertheless, he reckoned that he had needed every bit of his Sandhurst training to get them through and felt so proud, especially as the President of Pakistan came to see them. The final paragraph of Hugh's account reads as follows:

'In his replying speech the Brigadier [Jan Nadir Khan] admitted he had been apprehensive about our expedition plans in covering so much ground. But we had succeeded – and in doing so had established a new record. Such words were reward enough.

'The flight home the next day was long: fifteen hours. Each of us had time to reflect on the past month. We had learned a lot about the local people, of their spiritual values, their hospitality and their contentment in simplicity. We had learned also a lot about ourselves; the ability of the mind to overrule a body that says, "no more"; that an expedition is not about the survival of the fittest with the devil take the hindmost; it is about the strong helping the weak in the sure knowledge these roles can be reversed on the morrow. But our group had exhibited just that spirit and solidarity throughout and both were maintained to the end. No one grumbled about having to wait an extra half hour at Heathrow, as one boy's kit got delayed on the baggage carousel. All were determined to march out together to greet long-waiting and anxious parents, just as we had over the Thui An. At that moment I knew it had been my privilege to lead; Kelly would have been envious.'

Perambulations and Peregrinations

Aside from the expeditions, Hugh continued to journey around the world on his own account. The USA, Spain, Italy, Egypt, Syria, Pakistan, Holland, India and Bulgaria are just a few countries he explored. In 2002, he was invited to accompany an American lady friend on an uncharacteristically luxurious voyage – to New York on board the QEII.

John and Clara Semple, who knew Hugh well in Jeddah, Cairo and Khartoum, recalled the enjoyment Hugh took from the different and varied people he met on his travels. 'He particularly delighted in those he described as *gameen*, an Egyptian colloquial word he adopted, and adapted, to mean a congenial and

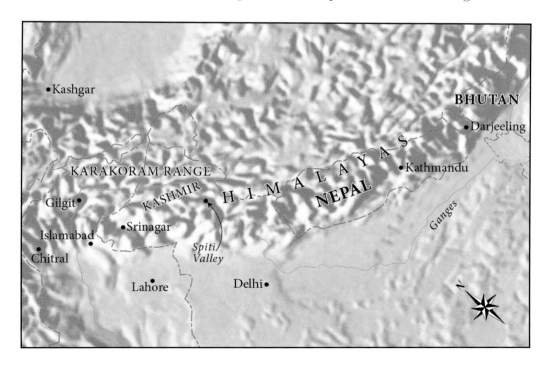

HRL and Harriet in Choumert Square.

amiable companion who, ideally, might also share his larky nature'.

Trevor Mostyn mentions the two overseas equine expeditions that Hugh undertook with Harriet Howard:

'Tall Hugh and small Harriet spent several months in 1984 and again in 1990 trekking remote areas of the Himalayas crossing streams with the [ponies and] donkeys by rope.'

Harriet relates that Hugh 'then became my truly greatest friend and, when he asked me on an expedition crossing the Himalayas to celebrate his 50th birthday, said it would be the nearest he would get to Heaven. Also, he told me he never took girls because they would want to powder their noses or find bushes. If I came, I could do neither and, if killed, I would be buried out there. I agreed to all.'

One of the many entertaining and revealing incidents that Harriet recalls (see Appendix F) went as follows: '...we were stopped by a woman who asked us in for tea. This we accepted and were led over a plank of wood, and two chairs were produced. Then the rest of the household came to say hello, and again we tried making conversation with everybody answering "Yes" to whatever. Hugh then said he had five children and I was his sister. Tea was produced with Hugh saying in a loud whisper, "Here goes cholera".'

Stephan Roman mentions another typical 'Hugh event' in 2004: '[His] wanderings led him to Transylvania where he celebrated his 70th birthday dancing the night away with a Hungarian Countess to the lively beat of a gypsy band and momentarily falling in love with a trapeze artist.'

Marian and Dave Hurle got their first glimpse of Hugh in Madeira: 'He was at the airport in full walking regalia, including huge boots, gaiters and shorts. He cut an imposing and unusual figure amongst the

HRL takes a break.

tourists! We soon discovered he was on the same holiday as us and as relative novices we thought it a good idea to walk together...We finished the holiday in Funchal, staying in a very smart hotel and enjoying some fine dining in our walking gear. Hugh's manners were impeccable, and he had a seemingly endless number of stories of the circus, his travels and his endless hunt for a suitable wife.'

Peter Clark recalls a visit Hugh made to him in Aleppo, Syria in 1993, recorded in his *Damascus Diaries: Life under the Assads*.

'Tuesday 25 May: I walk to the railway station and meet Hugh Leach, tall, pipe-smoking, alert. He has recently been camel riding in Sinai.

'Friday 28 May: Hugh and I wander along to an antique shop. We pass an ancient Citroen on the way. Now Hugh likes old cars and marvels at it. The owner is nowhere near, but Hugh opens up the bonnet and, to the encouragement of male passers-by, inspects the works. In the antique shop, he finds a bugle and, to the amazement of the shopkeeper, plays a Sudanese Reveille on it.'

There were many perambulations and peregrinations at home too. Every year, usually around the time of their birthday in May, Hugh and his twin sister Shirley would go on a walking holiday, sometimes at home, sometimes abroad, with a specific route in mind such as the West Highland Way, the Offa's Dyke Path or the trails of the Pyrenees.

Hugh used to say that he could easily live in a tent for the rest of his life. Even as a boy, he had wanted to camp. His elder sister Christine did too, but certainly not his father. Hugh couldn't explain why – even though he felt the cold and wore many layers, it was just 'in his blood'. Exmoor was a very regular destination. Martha would be packed to the gunnels with camping kit, tents, reading material etc. etc. and off they would head for Doone Country. At Halse Farm (near Winsford) he would settle into his habitual 'pitch', enjoying a week or two roaming the moors by day, reading and writing by lamplight at night.

Hugh's activities were briefly halted in October 2000 when he went into King Edward VII hospital in London to have the first of his two hip replacements.

Anne Harcombe recollects that naturally enough he took his bugle with him 'and played the Last Post each evening much to the amusement of the surgeon, Sarah Muirhead-Allwood, who also did my hip. So, I asked her if she remembered Hugh and his bugle, and she said, "How could I forget!"'

Harriet Howard tells of Hugh's and her holidays with pony and cart in Herefordshire, Yorkshire or Somerset, staying with friends or at B&Bs where

In his later years, HRL would take off for Exmoor with Martha and his well-appointed tent.

accommodation for a pony was possible '...the pony so often having better accommodation than us...Occasionally we would be taken for gypsies as we travelled with buckets hanging from the axle and hay nets tied to the back. Especially in a town on the Welsh border as groups of gypsies had been camping nearby. The shop doors would be shut as we trotted through the streets...Hugh being oblivious to it all concentrating on keeping his pipe alight.'

In between major events, there were ceaseless minor excursions and Hugh continued his pattern of splitting his time (his 'dual-life') between London and Hinton St George. Visitors to Somerset would be taken for substantial bicycle rides around the Somerset Levels. He would also take off around the country on the train and surprise friends; a ring on the doorbell would reveal Hugh wearing his plus-fours standing beside his ancient bicycle.

One typical evening in 2004 took him and his companions Norman and Marilyn Cameron and Sue Farrington on bicycles across the Levels from Hinton St George to Wells, where they enjoyed an evening of Middle Eastern reminiscing. Norman remarks: 'When it came to his anecdotes, one was not quite sure how much salt to administer, but they were all part of Hugh's fun.'

Anne Harcombe recalls a similar time: 'cycling over the Somerset Levels on [Hugh's] "Must-Have" 1930s Raleighs to hear choral evensong at Wells

HRL frequently accompanied Harriet Howard when she entered carriage-driving competitions.

Dr Tim Myatt: 'He was a warm, affable, intensely well informed, sprightly, mischievous sort of chap, with history in his fingertips and a twinkle in his eye.'

With his twin sister Shirley during one of their annual walks to celebrate their birthday.

Cathedral, and another time cycling over a stony Quantocks track in wind and rain and his bike getting not one but two punctures'.

It had pleased Hugh to find another distant kinsman on the Somerset Levels, who also claimed links with Northleach in Gloucestershire. John Leach, grandson of the 'father of British Studio pottery' Bernard Leach, lived at Muchelney, not ten miles from Hinton St George. By coincidence, John Leach is also a cousin of Will Facey, the publisher of Hugh's *Seen in the Yemen*.

MEDALS AND AWARDS

Martin Timmis: '…since he left the army, Hugh never forgot his former friends and colleagues, regularly attending reunions, and seldom missing marching to the Cenotaph each November with the regiment's Old Comrades, complete with his bowler hat and medals, or his "post-nominals" as he quaintly liked to call them. Hugh was extremely proud of his military connections.'

Opposite: In hiking mode.

HUGH
RAYMOND
LEACH
OBE, MBE (Mil)

5 MAY 1934 - 14 NOV. 2015

SOLDIER, DIPLOMAT,
TRAVELLER

"COLD HARD VOICES WHISPER AND SAY
HE IS CRAZED BY THE SPELL OF ARABIA
IT HAS STOLEN HIS WITS AWAY"

THE FINAL CHAPTER

In 2010, Hugh fell while cleaning out the fishpond in his garden at Brettingham Court, injuring his shoulder and knocking his confidence. After that he became increasingly anxious about where to base himself.

Running as a thread through it all was the continuing search for 'Mrs Leach' who would look after him. Friends listened as Hugh agonised over what his options might be. Should he consolidate in London? He wondered about buying the upper part of the house directly opposite his in Choumert Square – he had always loved the variety of the Square and Peckham; the many nationalities who lived in the neighbourhood; the cultural mix. But he felt he would miss the countryside if he moved permanently to London.

Soon after Hugh had decided that his Middle East archives should go to St Antony's, Oxford, a college specialising in international relations, an opportunity came up to rent an apartment very close to the college. The flat afforded a superb outlook over the 'dreaming spires' in one direction and towards the hills outside Oxford from the back. Having been brought up in nearby Abingdon, he felt he would be going home. Besides, it had the advantage of Harriet Howard's brother living on the floor above.

He put Brettingham Court on the market, and in 2012 it was all but sold, when Hugh changed his mind; the move was 'off', and his 'dual-life' continued.

However, 2014 was a turning point. The death of his elder sister Christine that year came as a great shock and, although the family joined together to celebrate Hugh and Shirley's eightieth birthday in May, by the end of September, he was no longer able to travel to London, or look after himself solely with the help of kindly neighbours and his cheerful cleaning lady, Helen, who had willingly taken on extra duties.

Opposite: HRL's headstone, Spring Road cemetery, Abingdon.

So it was that in 2015 Choumert Square was sold. In the event, Brettingham Court suited his requirements, having accommodation for a carer, local friends, and village facilities such as the community shop and his favourite establishment, Dorothy's Tea Rooms.

Support was needed with, initially, day care, and eventually live-in carers. He enjoyed visits from old friends, taking them to Dorothy's. Reluctantly he had to give up cycling, but continued a daily walk, even when using a walking frame.

His falls increased and in March 2015 it became necessary for him to move to a nursing home. After deteriorating, he was taken to Southmead Hospital in Bristol where he was diagnosed with progressive supranuclear palsy. In retrospect, this cruel condition had

St George's parish church, Hinton St George.

quite possibly been the reason for his fall in the fishpond. After discharge from hospital in Bristol in September, he spent his last weeks at a nursing home in Bath, where he died on 14 November 2015.

Jon Aldridge supplied an audio recording of Hugh proposing a vote of thanks to Bill Colegrave in 2011 after a lecture entitled 'Half Way to Heaven'. He points out that Hugh had 'mentioned a wish, if he should die abroad, for his ashes to be scattered in the Oxus to the sound of a reading of the last sixty lines of *Sohrab and Rustum* by someone from the Society or his old school.'

In the event, these words were read by Tony Howell, an Old Abingdonian (OA1960), at Hugh's funeral service at Hinton St George.

Apart from those in *The Times* and the *Telegraph*, obituaries appeared in his old school and regimental (both British and Omani) magazines, as well as those of other clubs and societies with which he was involved (for Sir Harold Walker's obituary in *Asian Affairs*, see Appendix G).

Having always maintained close links with the Royal Tank Regiment, it was particularly fitting that Hugh's memorial service took place at the Regiment's London church, St Mary, Aldermary, in the City of London, on 9 April 2016. Tony Howell reported in the *Griffen* that: 'the main floral arrangement incorporated Hugh's coffee pot, his bowler hat, and one of his trumpets. At the end of the service a trumpeter played John Stanley's "Trumpet Voluntary". It was a fitting closure to the life of a very distinguished Old Abingdonian.'

Extract from *Sohrab and Rustum*

So, on the bloody sand, Sohrab lay dead;
And the great Rustum drew his horseman's cloak
Down o'er his face, and sate by his dead son.
As those black granite pillars, once high-rear'd
By Jemshid in Persepolis, to bear
His house, now 'mid their broken flights of steps
Lie prone, enormous, down the mountain side—
So in the sand lay Rustum by his son.

And night came down over the solemn waste,
And the two gazing hosts, and that sole pair,
And darken'd all; and a cold fog, with night,
Crept from the Oxus. Soon a hum arose,
As of a great assembly loosed, and fires
Began to twinkle through the fog; for now
Both armies moved to camp, and took their meal;
The Persians took it on the open sands
Southward, the Tartars by the river marge;
And Rustum and his son were left alone.

But the majestic river floated on,
Out of the mist and hum of that low land,
Into the frosty starlight, and there moved,
Rejoicing, through the hush'd Chorasmian waste,
Under the solitary moon; – he flow'd
Right for the polar star, past Orgunjè,
Brimming, and bright, and large; then sands begin
To hem his watery march, and dam his streams,
And split his currents; that for many a league
The shorn and parcell'd Oxus strains along
Through beds of sand and matted rushy isles—
Oxus, forgetting the bright speed he had
In his high mountain-cradle in Pamere,
A foil'd circuitous wanderer—till at last
The long'd-for dash of waves is heard, and wide
His luminous home of waters opens, bright
And tranquil, from whose floor the new-bathed stars
Emerge, and shine upon the Aral Sea.

Matthew Arnold

On 1 December 2015 Hugh was buried in the Spring Road cemetery, Abingdon, the same cemetery as his parents, as he had requested. Inspiration for his headstone came in the shape of his parents' memorial. By removing, in imagination, the sundial on the top, the remaining pyramid reflected the Egyptian pyramids, in the shadow of which Hugh had spent some of his happiest days.

The inscription reads:

Hugh Raymond Leach, OBE, MBE (Mil)

5 May 1934 – 14 Nov 2015

Soldier, Diplomat, Traveller

"Cold hard voices whisper and say

He is crazed by the spell of Arabia

It has stolen his wits away"

Stephan Roman says: 'There could not be a more fitting epitaph for Hugh Leach, the soldier, diplomat and scholar. Although he loved his life in Somerset and Peckham Rye and his career with the Army and the Foreign Office, it was for Arabia that he longed and for the freedom, adventure and romance that the desert brought him.'

Rebecca Wilmshurst offers a final, personal, summary: 'For me, however, the Hugh I most recall is that of the kind, compassionate man who over the thirty years that I knew him shared with me one of life's greatest gifts: a trusting friendship that was understanding, unconditional, loyal, thoughtful and entirely generous.'

'A one-off, as they say, we shall not see his like again.'

Sir Roger Tomkys

Opposite: A favourite image of Hugh's with which he bade farewell at the end of *Seen in the Yemen*. Sana'a 1977.

Appendices

Appendix A

'A Bugler's Life'

A talk given by Hugh Leach: *First Person* BBC Radio 4
on 5 April 1990

Since I was not born within earshot of a regimental barracks where the stirring sounds of drum, fife and bugle would have been carried to my infant ear, I cannot account for how first those magical sounds stirred an atavistic chord. However, I can recall how lovingly I purchased my first instrument for five shillings, a battered B-flat bugle clearly stamped on its bell, Henry Potter & Co, Charing Cross Road, London, 1914. I can also recall repeated complaints of the neighbours as I learned to play it. As soon as I was able, I joined my school cadet force, volunteering as a bugler and also the school band where I graduated from 3rd to 2nd to 1st B-flat cornet under the expert tutelage of Mr …? from the Salvation Army. The bugle call that stirred me most was the fire alarm.

At cadet camp each summer I longed for there to be a fire so I could be the centre of an unfolding drama as I sounded this call from the four corners of the cantonment. At one such camp, near Aldershot in 1949, my world was collapsing as the final day approached and there had been no such demand on my prowess, so I conceived a plan. Near to our tent lines lay the straw store for our palliasse mattresses. In the early hours of the last day I crept from under the tent flap as if to attend the call of nature and lit my home-made fuse. Safely back in my tent I waited a couple of minutes and then nudged my snoring neighbour, 'Can you smell anything?' In a trice I was up, grabbed my bugle and clad only in boots, beret and pyjamas sounded the joyful music from every vantage point until my lungs felt they would burst. The effect was magical, a distinct flutter like a thunder flash being let off in the dovecote. Fortunately, no one ever discovered this, my first and last act of arson.

School led to Sandhurst and the regular army and more responsible military duties lay ahead, but my love of all forms of martial music never diminished. As Adjutant of my regiment, I tried to run the day's routine through bugle calls, but this was considered antiquated and met with opposition. Half-way through my career I transferred to the diplomatic service where, strangely, I was able to indulge this particular idiosyncrasy in greater measure.

One of my happiest postings was Egypt. I lived in a large rambling house at the foot of the Pyramids. Despite its twenty-one rooms I chose to sleep in a tent in the garden, for this meant at each morning I was woken by Egyptian buglers sounding Reveille from a nearby camp. They played the lovely Turkish Reveille, a relic of Ottoman rule. I ran the house routine on bugle calls, the thing I had failed to do in the army. Most useful of all, since the garden where we spent much of the time was large, I had devised a system whereby I could order drinks from outside. I composed separate tunes for the more familiar drinks, gin and tonic, whisky and soda, Stella beer and so on. The number required was indicated by the number of Gs at the end of each call. I taught these to one of the houseboys and, in this way, he was able to bring to the assembled guests the tray with their exact requirements.

Another memory carried from Cairo is that of riding in the desert under a full moon with my friend the Austrian countess who lived nearby. One such night was that of the annual dinner of the Attaché Corps and they had erected a large marquee in the sands. As we galloped past, throwing up clouds of dust I sounded the charge on the cavalry trumpet. A bevy of bristling moustaches appeared at the tent door and I was later told the Hungarian military attaché was so overcome with nostalgic animation he could hardly be restrained.

In the hot and torrid Sudan, each Christmas I would take my cornet from its dusty case and play Christmas carols outside the gaunt block which housed members of the East German mission, a secretary holding a hurricane lamp above my head on a broomstick. My rendering of *Stille Nacht* and other German carols would never fail to bring pale-faced *hausfraus* to the windows dabbing their eyes. Perhaps, mine was an early inroad into the days breaking down of east-west barriers, certainly my old Salvation Army tutor would have been pleased.

Over the years I have gathered an array of instruments. They now hang like a string of drying onions in the hallway of my home. They proudly carry their makers' names: a bugle I found in Peshawar, 'Hakim Din & Sons, Sialkot City'; another 'Rangar & Sons, New Delhi', and my favourite, a cavalry trumpet, given to me in Sana'a by an old Turk, Mr Turmash, the 75-year-old director of music of the Yemeni Army. It carried the Ottoman *tughra* of Suleiman the Magnificent and underneath rather incongruously 'Piletti, Milano'. Most convenient of all is a little German *Bunderpost* horn of perfect pitch which fits neatly into a knapsack and has accompanied me on my travels all over the world. A sunset call, First and Last Post and Reveille have been sounded in the great Nafud Desert in northern Arabia, in the step of Khorasan in northern Persia and to announce my 50th birthday dinner held at 14,000 feet at the foot of the Brahma glacier in the Himalayas. Most remote of all, I have sounded Reveille on a misty dawn on the banks of the Oxus, that great river which forms the border between Afghanistan and Russia, the ancient lands of Persia and Tehran, scene of the legend of Sohrab and Rustum. Did I not see the assembled armies of King Afrasiab and Peron Wiser emerging from his tent? What in fact I did see was the rather astonished Russian soldiers manning border watchtowers on the far bank of Soviet Badakhshan. The horsemen, cameliers, yak drovers and porters on these various expeditions have accepted such calls as 'boot and saddle' 'Hay up' and 'Litter Down' with uncomplaining, even if uncomprehending, equanimity.

But of all, my most moving experience was in Egypt. Each year in early November a remembrance service was held in the war graves cemeteries in El Alamein attended by visiting dignitaries and representatives from many missions. Traditionally the Egyptian Army provides the buglers but in early November 1973 in the smouldering aftermath with their own war with Israel, we could hardly ask them to stand for our dead when there were currently many of their own. A solution was devised whereby only the British and the Italian naval attachés, accompanied by the German Consul General in Alexandria, would carry out a simple wreath-laying ceremony at each of their three memorials. I would provide the music.

We drove to the Delta as the sun rose and picked up Herr Blomeier at Alexandria. At exactly 11 o'clock on the steps of the monument of the Commonwealth memorial at El Alamein I sounded the infantry Last Post, the notes carrying clear over the desert air. It was for me a singular moment; my regiment had taken a larger share of this decisive battle than in any other during the war. They paid a heavy price for their efforts. Many were buried in the neat rows of the graves below me. After two minutes' silence, I sounded the strident notes of the cavalry Reveille. The wreath-laying over, we drove through the desert the two miles across the line of the old minefield to the German memorial, a vast mausoleum, a *toten schloss*. Inside, the poignancy was not lost. I was now sounding for the German dead, those who

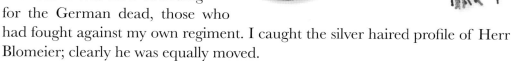

had fought against my own regiment. I caught the silver haired profile of Herr Blomeier; clearly he was equally moved.

A further mile on, we arrived at the Italian memorial. It had the air of a lofty cathedral, the dead seemingly placed in lockers. We climbed up onto the high balcony overlooking the interior and began the service. The acoustics were dramatic, the notes echoing from one wall to another as if a round was being played. In the middle of the two-minute silence an Italian priest, puffing and panting, entered below. He failed to notice us on the balcony above and hurriedly began to unpack his case of communion silver. As those first clarion notes of the Reveille rang out, there was a clatter as the astonished Father dropped his chalice on the marble floor. Poor man must have thought the last trumpet sounded.

As we drove back to Cairo, I thought how each of those memorials reflected the three national characters. The British one, its neat orderly rows of headstones set in the open amidst landscaped gardens; the German gaunt, lumpish, unyielding and yet, in its own way, equally moving and then the Italian. Exquisite architecture, though slightly racy, and that element, not of farce, just things going a little wrong. But I also thought of the unusual task thrust upon me, the privilege of sounding for the dead of opposing forces, now military allies, but thirty-one years earlier bent on each other's destruction. Then, more personally and humbly, I thought of how far I had come from that irresponsible act of arson a quarter of a century earlier at Aldershot, to this more responsible duty on the edge of the Libyan desert.

Appendix B

Vehicles

Cars

Hugh was proud to have been a member of the Automobile Association for over fifty years and of the Vintage Sports Car Club for fifty-seven years to 2012, when he sold Edwina. He was also a member of the Humber Register, the British Motorcyclists' Federation, and the Royal Enfield Owners' Club. One small irony is that despite his lifelong passion for motors, Hugh was well-known for becoming very car sick if anybody else was driving.

1927 Vauxhall 14/40 Princeton Tourer YE 2116

Bought in 1955 in Hugh's last term at Sandhurst and sold within a year when posted to Germany. Nevertheless, Hugh kept in touch with successive owners.

Wilhelmina: 1927 Humber 9/20 Tourer OT6968

Bought in 1956 just before Hugh went to Suez. The following year he had begun to restore her but, in order to buy Edwina, she was sold in pieces to Ian Crompton, who continued the restoration work. Again, Hugh kept in touch with the car's life.

Edwina: 1926 Humber 9/20 Tourer TX1852 (1058cc)

She only had two owners in eighty-three years. Bought for £20 in 1957, until 1967 she was Hugh's only car. Edwina remained a faithful companion until 2012 (see p.16).

Janette: Light 15 Citroen

Hugh paid £250 in Cairo for this car, which he bought from the Scottish widow of an Egyptian. He gave the car diplomatic plates and, eventually, after a ferry trip to Venice, drove her back home at the end of his posting in 1976. Once, when working without axle stands underneath this car, the jack holding it up collapsed. Luckily the wooden garage floor gave way and Hugh got away, very luckily, with a broken collar bone. In 1983, Janette was sold to Monica and John Macpherson, who are still her proud owners.

Martha: Series IIA Land Rover

Bought new for £810 in 1967, this vehicle was especially adapted with a white sun-reflecting roof, strengthened axles and rear springs for desert use. She won Land Rover's 'Search for a Legend' competition in 1998 – her prize being presented at Longleat by Lord Bath (pictured p.35). Martha was retired in 2014 and is now residing at Jaguar Land Rover Classic Works at Ryton, Coventry. Together she and Hugh had travelled over 250,000 miles.

Bikes

The list of Hugh's motorbikes is a long one: the first, a 98cc Cyc-Auto costing £43 had belonged to one of his schoolmasters, J B 'Piggy' Alston. Afterwards a more powerful 150cc Excelsior two-stroke, then his first 'proper' bike, a 250cc Royal Enfield. There followed a 250cc OK Supreme, a 350cc KSS Velocette, and a 350cc 3T Triumph twin, the most uninteresting as 'the wretched thing never broke down'. While serving in Libya, Hugh rode Matchless G3s when running the regimental motorcycle team.

After that came a Series C Vincent Rapide bought for £92 and sold by Sotheby's after twenty-five years for £7,500. Hugh's final motorbike (1993–2006) was an Enfield Bullet.

John Harding writes: 'In his motorbike collection was a monster, antiquated racing bike which he rode in T. E. Lawrence mode. Our daughters still talk about an outlandish apparition arriving at our house on Putney Heath clad overall in black leathers.'

On another occasion, similarly clad, he called unannounced at Thelma and Roy Vernon's farm in the Wye valley. 'He stayed for dinner, and the conversation ran on so late afterwards, that he stayed the night as well; we were grateful for our stock of airline toothbrushes.'

Hugh did not just have motorised bikes. He kept a stable of pushbikes, some dating from the 1920s. Suspecting, and unsuspecting, visitors would be led on long forays across the Somerset Levels, complete with Ordnance Survey maps, and wicker baskets. Invariably Hugh wore his plus-fours or, in the summer, empire-building shorts.

A Home on Wheels

While living at Nibley Green, Hugh bought his thirty-six foot long 1930 Brayshaw circus living wagon. Advertised for £500 in the *World's Fair* magazine, and equipped with bedroom, sitting room (with live fire), and kitchen, it needed complete restoration – which Hugh gave it. Only force of circumstance in 1995 caused him to part with it when he left Herefordshire.

Appendix C

COLLECTIONS

Musical Instruments

Hugh's collection of bugles and trumpets matched his passion for these instruments. He was never without an instrument wherever he went and, of course, was never to part with any that he had played.

His harmonium (circa 1887) was much travelled. In looking for memorials in Northleach, from where Hugh believed his family originated, he discovered it forgotten in a dusty schoolroom. Hugh asked the vicar if he'd take £5 and duly collected it in Martha. Surprisingly, Hugh couldn't read music and claimed he could only play it in 'C'.

Maps

Hugh's huge map collection reflected the geography of his career and retirement. He presented it to RSAA in his wooden map chest in 2014. Dr Rosie Llewellyn-Jones, the Society's archivist 2010-21, mentions that 'one of the most valuable maps was a fold-up map dated 1878 belonging to General Samuel Browne and annotated in ink with detailed routes to Kabul at the start of the Second Afghan War.' Another one of similar significance was an enormous 1872 map of the Nile River Delta commissioned by the Khedive of Egypt with captions in Arabic. The line of the newly completed Suez Canal features on it.

Also important is the large 'Wilfred Thesiger's Travels in Oman' map, drawn by Thesiger in 1969. The whereabouts of the original, once deposited at the Royal Geographical Society, is now unknown. The only other copy is lodged within Hugh's archive at St Antony's College in Oxford.

Carpets and Rugs

As might be expected, Hugh had a large collection of carpets, kilims (tapestry-woven rugs) and rugs, in both London and Hinton St George. However, a constant battle with moth meant that several, in particular saddle bags, such as the one pictured, have had to be destroyed.

Records

Hugh owned two wind-up gramophones and a collection of over three hundred 78-rpm records, ranging from military, classical, dance, trumpet, jazz, religious, vocal and Arabic to, strangely, 'The Teddy Bears Picnic'! He had several shelves of films on video cassettes (nothing digital in Hugh's world!) and just under two hundred self-recorded cassette tapes: bugle calls, radio programmes, Nine Lessons and Carols, music from the '20s and '30s, poetry, *Just William* etc. etc.

Items Arabian

Hugh's visitors were enchanted by the Arabian artefacts that decorated his houses. The list is long and varied and included: Yemeni spears, daggers, Arab chests, *jezails* (handmade rifles), alabaster oil lamps, coffee pots, camel saddles, brass and horn powder horns, communal mutton 'grab' bowls and camel milking bowls from Oman, Omani swords with a *tas* (shield made of whale skin), Qur'an stands, leather camel bags and an especial treasure: a saddle bag given to him by Freya Stark. He also had a number of doorstops and bookends made from pieces of the Hejaz Railway.

Appendix D

HOW RELIGIOUS TEXTS CAN BE CONVENIENTLY MISINTERPRETED

Text of address delivered by HRL at St George's Church, Hinton St George, Somerset on Remembrance Sunday, 13 November 2011

I guess many of you in the congregation today saw the Moviola film in the village hall last June entitled 'Of Gods and Men'. It was about a group of French Christian monks who ran a medical mission in the mid-1990s at Tibhirine, a remote mountain village in Algeria. It is based on a true story.

When a group of Muslim extremists were outside and about to attack them, the Chief Monk, named Christian, said 'Men never do so much evil as when they do it through religious conviction'. Alas true: so many wars have a religious motivation. And yet most religions preach peace. I thought that a good theme for what is, I think, my tenth such address, perhaps appropriate as this year is also the tenth anniversary of '9/11'.

In reality many, perhaps most, political and military leaders in history have used their clergy to adapt the meaning of scriptures to accord with the political and military circumstances of the time. Equally, there are numerous examples of clerics in most religions using the scriptures to justify military action against breakaway factions from the majority-accepted norm as being 'heretical'. The number of such within Christianity alone, from the 2nd century onwards, are numerous, with perpetrators being burnt at the stake. This is typically exampled by the Cathars or Albigensis, who were finally exterminated in the 14th century by the military might of the Inquisition. And yet our word 'heresy', which comes from the Greek *hairesis*, simply means 'to hold an opinion' or 'make a choice'. But it's conveniently taken on an evil pejorative meaning. In modern times Protestants and Catholics in Northern Ireland attack each other, whilst many similar sectarian conflicts such as that between the Sunnis and Shias exist in Islam.

Most serious wars from the start of the Christian era have been between the three Abrahamic religions: Judaism, Christianity and Islam, all of which are listed in the Qur'an as 'People of the Book to be respected'. Yet it's their texts that can be most easily misinterpreted. Who, for example, said, 'I come not to bring peace to the earth; I come with a sword'? Jesus, of course. There are various explanations as to what he meant, but none take it literally. Jesus was neither politician nor military commander; he remained a teacher. Muhammad on the other hand started as a teacher, then perforce became a politician and then a military commander. This profoundly affected the way Islam developed and why there are conflicting verses in the Qur'an depending on the circumstances of the time they were revealed. One even says, 'There is no compulsion in religion'.

The earliest wars between Christianity and Islam were the Crusades, those five wars between the 11th and 14th centuries for recovery of the Christian Holy Lands from Islam. Both sides were motivated by religion, whereas the reality was territorial.

Today the wars that concern us most are those where British soldiers are being killed. That was until recently Iraq, and currently Afghanistan, both countries where Islam is the principal religion. To further their causes, Muslim extremists, especially Al-Qaida, purposely misinterpret Qur'anic texts. For example, how often do we hear that much quoted verse 'Fight and slay the Pagans wherever you find them'. But this has nothing to do with Christians and Jews, who, as I've said, are mentioned in the Qur'an as 'People of the Book to be respected'. It refers to those desert Arabs who briefly converted to Islam when Muhammad was in Mecca in circa 620 AD, but soon got bored with it and, on returning to their tribal lands, apostatised and reverted to their old gods of the sky: the sun, moon and stars. They were known as *murtaad*, apostates. But today such texts are used to incite the killing of Christians.

All that despite Jesus having the highest place in the Qur'an after Muhammad himself, and Mary is mentioned more times in the Qur'an than in all the gospels put together. And rarely today do we hear this verse from the Qur'an (5:85) 'Closest to Muslims in love wilt thou find those who say "We are Christians", because they are devoted to learning and are not arrogant'.

Again, rarely do we hear how in 631 AD, the year before he died, Muhammad gave sanctuary in Medina to Christians fleeing extermination in the Yemen when that country was briefly under Jewish rule. And he allowed them to use his mosque as their church.

Muslim enmity towards the Jews on the other hand, subsequent to their being honoured as 'People of the Book', was occasioned by their refusing to aid Muhammad in Medina when, in 627 AD, the Muslims there were under large-scale attack from the people of Mecca. As a result, in that Battle of Uhud, the Muslims were defeated and Muhammad's uncle, Hamzah, was killed.

It's natural in war for both sides, whether of the same or differing religions, to call upon their deity for victory. In both world wars clerics on both sides convinced their soldiers that theirs was the just cause. And in the First both the British and Germans had virtually identical Christian emblems on their helmets.

Finally, we should remember that wars are started by politicians and then fought with amazing sacrifice and bravery by soldiers. So, along with thanking God for those latter, which is the main object of Remembrance Sunday, we might also pray that God gives wisdom to our political leaders to make the right decisions before committing us to war.

To conclude, let's look again at those words that the monk named Christian used at Tibhirine. 'Men never do so much evil as when they do it through religious conviction'. But, as we've seen, it's not so much religion itself that causes wars but political and military leaders who unashamedly use religion for their own motives. So perhaps Christian should have said, 'Men never do so much evil as when they do it through a deliberate misinterpretation of religious conviction for their own ends'.

Appendix E

SIR WILFRED
THESIGER KBE DSO
1910 – 2003

A tribute by HRL, one of a number by RSAA members in *Asian Affairs*, vol. XXXV, no.1, March 2004

Like others who had served among the bedu of Oman or the hill tribesmen of the Yemen frontier, to us the man behind *Arabian Sands* was a living legend. For me that legend was first brought into reality in the mid-1960s. Thesiger was travelling with the Royalist forces in the mountains of Yemen, engaged in a struggle with the Egyptian-supported Republic, and I was serving in our Embassy in Jeddah to where he regularly retired. Ever the profound raconteur, his tales of the fighting were laced with a sound military judgement. It was the

start of an intermittent friendship that lasted over three decades.

Ironically, our first chance to travel together was back in the Yemen, where I was posted, just ten years later. As with others who have lived with the desert Arab, Wilfred found his mountain cousin too devious and after a tour of the Highlands we were both happier descending to the lowland Tihama. We spent happy days shooting for the pot and peaceful nights under the stars. But as time went by, Wilfred became strangely withdrawn. I felt he needed space, so arranged for a couple of donkeys and their handlers to take him the five-day trek back up to Sana'a, whilst I went on elsewhere.

On return he was profound in his apologies. He had come direct from northern Kenya and before leaving Maralal had closed down his little household of Samburu adoptees, having decided to end his African days. He was already having the most bitter regrets for he now realised that he was saying goodbye to the sort of travel we had been doing with our chosen local friends. At sixty-seven he was too young for that and was already making plans to go back to Kenya and resurrect, so far as he could, his Samburu companions, which he subsequently did. However, it must be said there was within this  arrangement the inherent danger of injecting into a society modern forms of transport (his Land Rover) and more money than they were used to. This, the antithesis of Wilfred's shibboleth, 'I hope that by my coming nothing has been changed.'

Our next travels were a few years later in the Sudan, where I was then serving. Although his early years had been spent in Darfur Province, he was shocked to see how the country had deteriorated. He later agreed with me that Egypt, despite its teeming masses, had somehow retained a seductive charm, while the Sudan he had known had lost its collective soul. However, the people remained as warm as ever and the elders in Kutum, his old Headquarters, still told stories of how before going off on a lion shoot, he would say, 'If I'm killed, don't let them eat my head. They can have the rest.'

Wilfred Thesiger was not an academic Arabist in the tradition of St John Philby or Bertram Thomas. But his limited Arabic, mainly gained over the years by a sort of osmosis, had served him well. The Bedouin working vocabulary is small and one can communicate without too many words. I recall how, travelling in the Yemen, we were approached by a small boy, obviously in pain from a circumcision operation that had gone wrong. Wilfred inspected the damage and fumbled in his medicine chest for the remedy, which he handed to the youth. In all this consultation, diagnosis, prescription and instructions for usage not a single word had been spoken by either side. He was proud of his medical skills, especially in circumcision, for which he had been applauded on Kenyan Radio.

It is said Thesiger had no sense of humour. This was not true. But it was a dry one. Given the circumstances he was able to laugh at himself. He knew of his reputed toughness enshrined in the legend of his meeting Eric Newby and Hugh Carless in the Hindu Kush. But if a camp bed, pillow or mosquito net was available, he used them – usually pinching the best! Similarly, if a Land Rover broke down, he would put an enquiring nose under the bonnet. On such occasions a slow smile would break his cracked features indicating he knew just what you were thinking.

While his travel writing has rarely been surpassed, he never gave of himself in his letters. His hand was small but legible and fitted his economy of words. Unlike those of T. E. Lawrence or Freya Stark, they were not written for posterity. He read widely. Apart from the obvious Conrad or Buchan, his favourites included Mary Renault and Harold Nicolson.

All explorers, and especially Arabian ones, have a sensitivity about others they regard as trespassing on their patch. Wilfred's rancour was reserved especially for women travellers. He knew that both Freya Stark and Violet Dickson were visitors of mine in Arab capitals and he lost no time in expressing his views. But I teased him that both were very much kinder about him than he was about them. He was equally concerned lest other explorers should write about himself and did his best to prevent Michael Asher's recent biography appearing, preferring that should be done by his own appointee. He admitted he was quietly thrilled when people came up to him in the street, even supermarkets, to ask, 'Aren't you Wilfred Thesiger?' But the face helped!

He had a wonderful Victorian sense of etiquette. If the ambassador would join us for a meal or drink, despite any previous familiarity he would always make the point of rising to say, 'Goodnight to you, Sir'. For, as he said, the ambassador was the Queen's representative and in so doing he was saying goodnight to the Sovereign whom he held in high regard.

He valued his friends but I doubt if any of them really knew him intimately. As was said of Lawrence, he kept them in separate drawers, pulling out one at a time when the mood suited. Like Philby he could be querulous and moody, but equally kind, courteous and charming, all of which later increased with the mellowness of age.

I do not personally take the view there is no more exploration to be done. But surely no one will have the opportunity to explore and record the now vanished world of pre-oil Arabia in the way he did so brilliantly both in prose and with black-and-white photography. *Ma'a salaamat Allah.*

Appendix F

ON EXPEDITION WITH HUGH IN THE WESTERN HIMALAYAS

Harriet Howard writes graphically of her expeditions with Hugh. In the context of this book, it is impossible to do justice to the many perils and pitfalls which they faced, especially on their second expedition. A few 'snapshots' from Harriet's diary must suffice, together with the following introduction:

I felt very honoured to have accompanied Hugh on two expeditions across the Western Himalayas, and then a third trip to Darjeeling and Assam. He became my truly greatest friend and, when he asked me on an expedition crossing the Himalayas to celebrate his fiftieth birthday, said it would be the nearest he would get to Heaven. Also, he told me he never took girls because they would want to powder their noses or find bushes. If I came, I could do neither and, if killed, I would be buried out there. I agreed to all.

Staying on the houseboat [at Srinagar in Kashmir] each evening, Ahmed Baktoo came to go through the maps as decisions were made as to the routes to be taken. One pass in the Pir Panjal, the Margan Pass, he thinks will be impassable with the snows. He keeps saying that it is the wrong time of year for these things, but Hugh persuades him it is most important...

It being April the pass had many feet of snow, so Hugh announced a 3.30 a.m. start with a bugle call. Porters and ponies ready, on we climbed. The pony men and porters were all sending messages and whistling back and forth to each other. At the top we decided not to cross as it was too dangerous for the ponies as their hooves would go straight through the snow. Back down we went, but Hugh was not to be defeated. Next morning, we had exchanged eight ponies for twenty-seven porters!

I did say to Hugh that it seemed a lot of people and animals involved for just the two of us. He explained when you are tackling mountains in freezing conditions the dangers must be taken seriously. Mountains, like deserts, are played with at your peril. Food, provisions and shelter have to be carried for at least three weeks as there is no hope of replenishment.

Crossing the Margan was our hardest time. Known as the Dead Man's Pass, it had taken many lives! A man had fallen and only his head was showing. Luckily our men found him just in time. I kept sinking and falling on my knees longing to be flat and go to sleep on the snow. Hugh kept me going. He said afterwards that if I had lain down, I could have been in a coma in ten minutes and then dead not long after...

Many a time passing through villages that had not seen many, if any, Westerners we would have a trail of children following, especially with Hugh being six foot four and me being four foot two. Hugh would always entertain them. One time he started to eat grass, which gave them fits of giggles. Another, he always carried matches for his pipe and would strike one on a stone to light. This they thought was real magic.

A new lot of ponies and mules were found from Inshin village. I always rode when possible and Hugh walked, reversing the Muslim tradition: man riding and woman walking behind! Hugh always said mules and ponies were much nicer to travel with than porters. They do not suddenly go bolshie with you and want more money in the middle of nowhere. The atmosphere is so much better with animals and pony men around. The one thing you have to watch out for are protruding rocks, as with their bulging loads they could so easily be tipped over the edge. The horsemen are looking out for them all the time. They run back and forth adjusting loads and even unloading at certain places. At one time, going up some rocks, one did go over backwards. The load acted as a cushion when she landed. A previous trip, Hugh lost one in a river but, for us, all ended well...

The whole expedition was by way of a celebration of Hugh's fiftieth birthday on 5 May. There would be a surprise event in the evening, although Hugh knew exactly what was going on, Shabaan and I exchanging loaded whispers about it. He was to bake a cake with fifty candles on top, which I had brought from England. We reached the village of Kharr (Kiar Nallah) and set up camp on the other side. Abdul Magid and I were told by Shabaan to keep Hugh away for half an hour so all the decorations, which they had been making secretly the night before, could be put up. The locals thought it was a wedding.

The campfire was lit to give a blaze of light and after dinner Abdul Aziz started a Muslim incantation calling upon *Allah* to grant us a long life and happiness. This was enjoyed by pony men as well.

As we travelled on, over the next few days we passed many Bakrwaal people on the move with their animals. There were great traffic jams on the narrow rocky ledges as hundreds of their goats would try and fit past us, with pack animals all clambering over the rocks. Our ponies luckily stood stock still...

We were nearing Padmar and our expedition was coming to an end...Abdul Magid and Shabaan had managed to bribe a bus driver to bring an empty bus to pick us and all the luggage up to return to Srinagar. After loading us up at 4 a.m., he drove to the station to pick up all the passengers. There were many hazardous moments during the fourteen-hour journey...

Arriving in Delhi seemed like stepping into an oven: 107°F (42°C). But when we came off the plane Hugh decided to go round the airport telling everybody how cold it was! He takes out his heavy tweed *pheran** and puts it on, creating great sideways looks. By now the security guards were looking very suspicious, almost cocking their guns. The rest of the passengers had walked off to the airport buildings. As he was trying to get the *pheran* over his head the guards were now thinking he was fiddling with a gun. At last, it was on and we both walked alone to the building, Hugh still saying how cold he was.

Six years later in 1990 we were to venture again...for three months and carrying on from where we left off. We went up to Srinagar against advice because of all the troubles...At the airport there was a mass of armed soldiers and police... Everywhere was tense and the streets deserted which are normally full of people. We came to more army check points – eleven in all, each one getting worse as we got nearer in. Most of the soldiers had been brought in from the south and hated the Muslims here. They were bored and undisciplined; at one of the checks the

* *Pheran*: traditional woollen full-length Kashmiri over-garment.

125

officer in charge just sat by the side letting them do anything. Their guns seemed much too free, being held towards us with no proper control on the trigger end.

The soldiers would insist the baggage was taken from the back of the jeep and opened. Hugh did this in his marvellously slow manner, and took out his pipe and lit it, then carefully undid the ropes that were keeping our bags together. When they came across his bugle they shouted "What's that!"...

Eventually we arrived at the houseboat; our host Ahmed awoke that morning to find it surrounded by machine guns. There were burnt out buildings everywhere, cross firing each night and bombs going off. Soldiers were searching for guns and rebels, pulling everything apart. One night when we were there, beatings were happening, women were being raped and many men killed.

We were about the only Europeans, and we felt so sorry for the Kashmiri people...The problem now was, having got in, how to get out. So, with the help of Hugh's Kashmiri friends, we ran the gauntlet of curfew. We made for Kishtwar, one hundred and thirty miles south, where we finished our last expedition.

Our car journey had many difficulties with landslides, unsafe bridges and river crossings. Our hearts sank; there had just been another rockfall over the road ahead and in no way could we pass. Farouk managed to find six men from nowhere. They were about to try and remove every rock. But Hugh suggested that, if he had a platoon of soldiers, he would have had them make a ramp over the rocks. This was carried out with great success. We next came to a deep, rushing mountain stream. Would it be too deep for the jeep? Or should we risk driving over a very weak bridge. Farouk waded the stream to see how deep it was then decided to have a go, hoping no water would get in the exhaust. But

first the luggage was unloaded and carried over the bridge so the vehicle would be lighter. Luckily Mushtaq managed to get over without stalling.

We had not driven far when it all had to be unloaded again as there was one very steep hill ahead. The luggage would have to be carried up the hill. By now we had created quite an audience. All men and village boys came to help carry and also push the jeep up the hill. I think Hugh doing most of the pushing...The next day there was to be a

7 a.m. start to reach Shoel, many times loading and unloading the ponies as the ledges were too narrow and the packs could tip the animals over if they hit the sides. Over glaciers, taking care not to fall under and never be seen again. Then the avalanches, hoping they would not come down on top of us!

Crossing glaciers there was a lot of encouragement needed to get the animals across. One had to cross a narrow ledge of snow onto sheer ice, which in places had melting holes into the darkness below. The first pony was so frightened they had great trouble getting it onto the ledge, also the mule behind with the tents. Such a relief when eventually they were all over.

Later I suddenly saw two children running terrified. It turned out they had seen Hugh in his shorts. It may have been the first white man they had ever seen!...

I had a dream saying I was going to die and insisting it was going to be soon; it was all in his book. But luckily Hugh had a dream that an air-conditioned coach had come to pick us up.

Later we set up camp at Pindu which was full of Nepalese workers from over the border. The pony men and our men were exhausted so great arguments between them. No one knew what to do. The pony men wanted to go back, so now we would be left. How will we get out of here? The next morning men from the village turned up to discuss porters to get us to Purthi as it was totally impossible for ponies. So the pony men were to leave us. We had fond farewells and they waved and waved till out of sight...More depression in our camp about getting out. As Hugh says, we were hostages to the people and they can ask anything to porter us out.

Farouk and Abdul Salam are getting more silent. Some Nepalese porters appeared but wanted too much money...All afternoon Hugh and I thought of the wonders of home and gave each other messages for our families if one or other never got back.

A few more days of glaciers and rock falls. Our loyal guide Farouk was very down and worried. And Abdul Salam our faithful cook raises his hands to Heaven and says it is the most difficult trip he has had to do. He tells me how he likes Sahib (Hugh) but has had many Memsahibs who complain.

At the top of the Rohtang pass, our porters went bolshie and said they wanted more money, so a near fight between them and Farouk. Poor Farouk and Salam both looking shattered at the worry of it all. Both saying it was the most difficult trek, every day a worry!...

Later that night when we had driven to Manali by jeep we discovered the

porters had stolen many tins of food – that's why they were holding back. They had taken the tins out and hidden them for when they returned. Also, paraffin had been spilt over Hugh's *pherans*.

Hugh discovered a marvellous way to move on the many children surrounding our camp. He would put his fingers to his lips saying 'swoosh', then prayed with his hands. They straight away thought he was meditating and went away.

Bob Newbury was to help us in the next part of our journey. A friend of his turned up and was amazed how we had survived the last part as he thought it was very dangerous.

We were to leave the Parbatti Valley to visit Malana – a remote village at 10,000ft which is only accessible a few months a year, after a steep climb and impassable to pack animals. Horses are not allowed. Police and government officials rarely set foot in so remote a place. It claims to be one of the oldest democratic republics in the world...It is very much a caste system and we foreigners are untouchable. On the climb up we met a group of Malana women who were very interested in us, but as soon as Hugh went near, they ran. As we approached the village, we had to hide our leather shoes as leather was banned. If we had gone in with leather, we would have to buy a goat and sacrifice it.

We had to walk in the middle of the streets and not touch the walls either side. Otherwise [again] a goat to be sacrificed.

We camped by the River Tirth near Manguleur. The next morning a mass of children, on their way to school, flocked around the tents very interested. They could not get over Hugh as he started playing the fool looking a real idiot. Then he took the bugle out and played it and they thought he was wonderful. Rather like the Pied Piper.

At one camp Hugh put his tent up on the edge of a steep bank that went straight down to the rushing river below. If he goes out in the night and turns right instead of left it will be the end of him. Also, I hoped there would not be a storm in case the whole thing blew over the edge...

We climbed more into the snow leaving the tree line behind, the clouds all around us as we searched for our route. The toughest day was to come; Hugh even prayed before we started. Up and up we went, rocks and snow alternately. Unexpectedly the ponies came to soft snow and fell into it one by one, but managed to be heaved up...At last, we reached the top. The scenery was like another planet. As Hugh said, 'Some of the peaks never conquered!'

The next day we came to a rock face with no sign of getting across without a rope. There was a sheer drop and one raging *nalla* with no hope of living. Shir Singh produced a rope which was put around my waist. As I started, Hugh noticed he (Shir Singh) was only holding the other end so if I had slipped, he would not have been able to hold me. Then Hugh took over. He put the other end around himself and then wedged himself in between the rocks so he could take a good hold. I prayed so hard as I'd never been so near death – a relief when I got to the other side of the face. Then the prayers started again watching the others come. Thank God for Hugh and the rope!

Hugh and I plus our great guides went on towards the Baralacha Pass: all day up and down clambering over scree with four-inch ledges. One slip down to the Chandra River...then a four-hour trek to the next river crossing at Tokpo Yongma – this was to be much more difficult...We met up with another group so Kaushal from our lot and Fuya from the other crossed together, with ropes around their waists in case they were swept away. Now there was to be a cavalry stampede. It was decided I was to be on one of the ponies. All the men shouting

to encourage them straight across otherwise they would be swept over. Shir Singh helped me by pushing mine from the side to keep it straight. The other worry was unseen holes in the riverbed or ponies pushing one over. Cheers as we reached the other side. Now Hugh's turn, it was thought better in pairs. All going well until they reached the deep faster bit and then the man with Hugh dropped his stick. Hugh then took his hand off the rope to try and pick it up, whereupon he fell over and all the air was taken out of his lungs. He managed to get up, with all on the bank yelling 'leave the stick'. A relief to see him safe.

The next day was to get to the Baralacha Pass – about 16,400 feet. At the top there was a small sort of temple where our men made Hugh and I scratch our names, by other names, on a piece of slate. Then Hugh played his bugle, hoping to be the highest bugle player!! Sonam salutes as he plays. It was quite a sight.

Our third Indian journey took place in 1998–9 when we spent a month in Darjeeling and Assam. Christmas was celebrated in the iconic long-established Windamere Hotel, before less dramatic touring in Assam, including travelling on the Darjeeling Himalayan railway 'toy train' and searching for rhino from the back of elephants in the Kaziranga National Park. No 'alarums and excursions'! Although less adventurous than our two previous expeditions, it was nevertheless a delightful culmination to our Indian travels.

Appendix G

HUGH LEACH OBE MBE (MIL)
5 MAY 1934–14 NOVEMBER 2015
Obituary by Sir Harold Walker KCMG from RSAA Journal
Asian Affairs, vol. XLVII, no.1, March 2016

Hugh Leach, at the time one of the Society's two Honorary Vice-Presidents, died on 14 November after a long illness. The funeral took place on 30 November at Hinton St George, Somerset, and Hugh was buried the next day at Abingdon, the place of his birth.

Hugh was a man of many parts: soldier (1955–1967), diplomat (1967–1982), Arabist, traveller and explorer, photographer, circus owner, scholar, author. In retirement he had two homes, one in Hinton St George and one in Choumert Square, Peckham Rye. In both he played a prominent role, whether in terms of the life of the community or in terms of the community's relations with the authorities.

Hugh was an undisguised romantic. In an article about his time in Oman for the magazine of Abingdon School, of which he always remained a loyal and contributory member, he wrote: 'Much has been written in romantic vein about the "desert and the stars" – it's all true! The joy of spending nights in utter solitude or with the Bedouin must be among the most rewarding things in life'. He was given to the great outdoors. *En poste* in Cairo between 1972 and 1976 he had a sizable house near the pyramids; being Hugh he did not sleep in the house but rather in a tent in the garden. It was the same in others of his postings. He was not suited to head office: when tired or bored he would stretch out on his desk and go to sleep, puzzling the secretaries.

It was all of a piece that he was fond of dressing up. Towards the end of his time with the Royal Tank Regiment, into which he was commissioned in 1955, there was a requirement for a military history presentation: Hugh dressed up as Manstein while another officer was Rommel. On another occasion he invited some fellow officers to travel with him in his Land Rover from Catterick to Newcastle to see a play. On the way back on the A1 he pulled into a lay-by, laid out a carpet and proceeded to serve little cups of Arab coffee to his companions. Generally, he used drama to enliven the talks he gave to colleagues – or church congregations.

In the course of his life Hugh owned a Norton motorbike and a 1926 Humber 9/20 tourer called Edwina. But it was Martha, the Series IIA Land Rover, with a quarter of a million miles on the clock, that won the company's 'In Search of a Legend' competition, on the occasion in 1998 of the 50th anniversary of the make. To the irritation of friends, Hugh never moved into the information technology age. He wrote long screeds in small not always neat handwriting, often larded with a few words of Arabic in neater Arabic script. But it would be wrong to call him a technophobe: he serviced Martha himself.

Along with the romanticism Hugh preserved a boyish streak. He would not close his eyes at night without reading a chapter or two of the *Just William* stories by Richmal Crompton. He had a great love of the circus. In 1972 he took a part-share in a circus called the Circus Americano. He adopted the soubriquet Captain Leopold Lazard, MBE. When he was posted to Cairo he invited some of his former colleagues to work with the Egyptian State Circus, under the name Circus Britannia. This prompted the unhelpful headline in the *Daily Express* 'British Envoy Joins the Circus?' However, his Ambassador thought that Circus Britannia, which toured the Nile Valley, was a welcome enhancement of the UK's cultural appeal. Hugh later became an associate board member of the Academy of Circus Arts, a circus training school. Wherever he went Hugh used his bugle to effect. In 1973 he played the Last Post and Reveille at all of the British, German and Italian memorials at El Alamein when the Egyptian Army were unable to provide the buglers for the annual commemoration.

Hugh had a quirkish sense of humour. In a lecture to the Royal Society for Asian Affairs on 3 January 1991 entitled "From the Upper Indus to the Sutlej" he recorded that 'Shortly after daybreak on my birthday I had heard the strident note of the Himalayan cuckoo and was moved to write to *The Times* asking whether this was a record so early on one's quinquagenary. Following local tradition, I used as paper the bark of the bhojpatra tree, a birch, *Betula utilis*, which is common on the tree line around 12,000 feet. My letter would have been carried by local mail runners who ply between the villages, making the outward journey one day and the return the next…' I have not been able to ascertain whether the letter was delivered.

Hugh's life was, however, far from being all a matter for amusement. On the contrary, his army life was deadly serious. His tank was the first to be landed at

Port Said in the Suez operation of 1956. At least three times while he was Desert Intelligence Officer in Nizwa, Cairo Radio reported the death of Captain Leach. Evidently the impact of Hugh's operations was sufficient to attract the attention of the enemy's propaganda, but mercifully an inaccurate attention.

Hugh's interest in exploration and travel was also deep and serious. He recorded, in 'A Ride to Shiwa: A Source of the Oxus', a lecture given to the Society on 22 April 1986, that in the Fourth Form at Abingdon School he had been required to learn Matthew Arnold's poem *Sohrab and Rustum*. Ever since that time it had been an ambition of his to read it on the banks of the Oxus, and to explore the source of the river. He eventually achieved his ambition. He argued convincingly that the true source of the Oxus is Lake Shiwa. In the Society's records is a photograph of Hugh reading the poem on the south-west bank of the river.

He recorded separately that in his will he had left instructions that his ashes should be scattered in the Oxus while the last sixty lines of *Sohrab and Rustum* were read.

Generally, he loved exploration and travel, particularly in the Himalayas and Central Asia. While posted to Sana'a (1976–1977) he climbed the tallest mountain in the country, Jabal Nabi Shu'ayb, a demanding climb; he reached the top ahead of his younger companion. In the Yemen he was particularly proud of an expedition he made to find a still extant Jewish community near Sa'dah.

Hugh joined the Royal Society for Asian Affairs on 11 July 1962 and first became a Member of Council in 1983, while still in government service. The rules require that Council Members must step down after two stints. But Hugh's services were so valuable that eventually the post of Society Historian was created in order that Hugh could always attend Council meetings. The Society's website records that between 1980 and 2009 he wrote fourteen learned articles for *Asian Affairs*, covering such matters as the ride to Shiwa already mentioned, a journey to the source of the Jaxartes, and the strategy and tactics of Lawrence of Arabia. He gave the Society many books and maps. In 1998 he was awarded the Society's Lawrence of Arabia Medal 'in recognition of his work of outstanding merit in exploration and research, both in Arab countries and the north-western part of the sub-continental countries…' Hugh was immensely proud of this award.

An outstanding achievement for the Society was the centenary history he wrote with the assistance of Sue Farrington, as she then was – *Strolling About on the Roof*

RSAA Centenary Dinner at the Savoy Hotel 15 May 2001. Clockwise from HRL: Mrs Elisa Chait, Captain Val Bailey RN, Sue Farrington, Sir Nicholas Barrington, Mrs Jenny Steger, Norman Cameron, Mrs June Bailey, Adrian Steger, Mrs Marilyn Cameron.

of the World (RoutledgeCurzon, 2003). Hugh also wrote *Seen in the Yemen: Travelling with Freya Stark and Others* (Arabian Publishing, 2011). The book is evocatively illustrated with photographs taken by Hugh's beloved Leica; a collection of some of the original photos may be seen in the library of the Society.

Towards the end of his government service the authorities gave Hugh the task of researching contemporary trends in Islam. He wrote a tome for official use, noting the increasing radicalisation of intelligent young Muslims. In a lecture to the Society on 27 June 1989 he warned that the rise of Islamism among Muslim emigrants to Europe might lead to racial problems. His researches into Islam led him also to become something of an expert on the Assyrian Church of the East. Altogether he became a learned scholar – one friend called him a polymath – but mercifully retaining the facility to write plain English.

Hugh never married, though he was often to be seen in attractive female company. He referred to his cottage in Choumert Square and his Humber Edwina as the only wives he could countenance.

More generally he was the most gregarious of men. He had no side, little concern with hierarchy. He liked to get to know people by living among them. In Hinton St George he never locked his door, ascribing his habit to Arab tradition. In Peckham Rye he would visit the market and the mosque to chat with local people. By the same token he liked to share his knowledge. He led many expeditions to the Himalayas, including expeditions of young people from the Society and Abingdon School. These expeditions were sometimes quite testing, not to say character-building; not all the young people appreciated rising early to the summons of Reveille on Hugh's bugle.

His sharing of his experiences arose from a generosity of spirit. He wanted others, particularly the young, to share what he himself found of value. The word 'inspiration' has often been used in tributes to him. A fellow officer wrote recently of a time in the '60s; a tall, fair-haired Captain, Hugh Leach, had recently rejoined the Regiment in the capacity as Adjutant after a period of service with local troops in Arabia. He introduced me to the enormous possibilities for secondment that existed in the Army at the time and fired up my enthusiasm for adventure. It was not long before I was poring over the vacancies in the Army's Secondment Manual to see the positions for which I might be qualified. Similarly, a former student at Abingdon School has written that a talk Hugh gave at the school, followed by his taking part in the Society's first Young Persons Expedition, 'shaped the rest of my life'; the person concerned went on to carve out a career in Asia.

Hugh Leach – a quirky man who served his country well; in the words of Matthew Arnold's *Sohrab and Rustum* a 'circuitous wanderer' (perhaps not so foil'd); a learned man; a generous man; a man who had the capacity to inspire. That is how the Society will remember him.

Appendix H

PUBLICATIONS

The range of Hugh's interests was and is reflected in his writings. The list below consists in large part of items published in *Asian Affairs*, the journal of the Royal Society for Asian Affairs (RSAA). Although not exhaustive, examples of his other writings follow.

Books

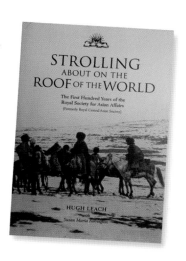

Strolling About on the Roof of the World. The First Hundred Years of the Royal Society for Asian Affairs [formerly Royal Central Asian Society] by Hugh Leach with Susan Maria Farrington (RoutledgeCurzon 2003) ISBN 0-415-29857-1.

[This book provides a fascinating detailed and illustrated record of the origins, history and people of the Society.]

Reviews appeared in: *Asian Affairs, Bulletin of the Association of the Study of Travel in Egypt and the Near East* (ASTENE), *Bulletin of the Military Historical Society, Chowkidar, Indian Army Association Newsletter, Journal of the Sultan's Armed Forces, Literary Review* and *Pennant.*

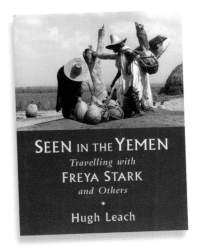

Seen in the Yemen. Travelling with Freya Stark and Others by Hugh Leach (Arabian Publishing 2011) ISBN 978-0-9558894-5-5.

[Hugh's enthusiasm for black-and-white or sepia photographs and for the use of his Leica cameras found expression in this book.]

Reviews appeared in: *Asian Affairs, Bulletin of the British Foundation for the Study of Arabia (BFSA), Geographical Magazine, Saudi Aramco World, The British-Yemeni Society Journal, The Saudi Gazette* and *The Spectator.*

Articles in *Asian Affairs*,
the Journal of the RSAA

'A Ride to Shiva: A Source of the Oxus', Vol. 17 no.3 (1986) pp.264-276.
(based on the illustrated lecture HRL gave to the Society on 22 April 1986)
'Observing Islam from within and without', Vol. 21 no.1 (1990) pp.3-19.
(printed text of lecture to the Society 27 June 1989)
'From the Upper Indus to the Sutlej: Alarums and excursions along the Indian Himalaya', Vol. 22 no.3 (1991) pp.330-336.
'From the Himalayas to the Hindu Raj: The Society's First Young Persons' Tour. July 18 - August 16, 1992'. Vol. 24 no.2 (1993) pp.145-156.
'Racing Kelly Across the Roof of the World', Vol. 27 no.1 (1996) pp.45-52.
(an account of the Abingdon School expedition, 16 July-16 August 1994)
'Murder at Caxton Hall. The Society's Involuntary Legacy of Amritsar', Vol. 29 no.2 (1998) pp.81-183. [The article drew on material from *The Amritsar Legacy: Golden Temple to Caxton Hall. The Story of a Killing* by Roger Perkins (Picton 1989)].
'A Journey to the Sources of the Jaxartes', Vol. 30 no.3 (1999) pp.269-283. [an account of a journey by four members of the Society: Hugh Leach, Adrian Steger, Isobel Shaw and Sue Farrington]
'Junior Members' Meeting 1999', Vol. 30 no.3 (1999) pp.365-367.
'Lawrence's strategy and tactics in the Arab Revolt', Vol. 37 no.3 (2006) pp.337-341. [reprinted from the October 2005 issue of *History Today* by permission of the editor]
'From Bavaria to Bokhara to Isle Brewers: The Extra-ordinary Life and Times of Dr the Revd Joseph Wolff DD', Vol. 38 no.3 (2007) pp.318–316.

Obituaries in *Asian Affairs*

'Colonel Sir Hugh Boustead KBE CMG DSO MC', Vol. 11 no.3 (1980) pp.359–60. [The final sentence of the text might be applicable to Hugh Leach himself: 'Gabriel is in for a leg-pull too.' We can imagine the two of them plotting over a bowl of ambrosia…]
'John Burke da Silva, CMG', Vol. 34 no.3 (2003) pp.371–372.
'Sir Wilfred Thesiger KBE DSO', Vol. 35 no.1 (2004) pp.38–39.
'Colonel David de Crespigny Smiley LVO OBE MC and Bar', Vol. 40 no.2 (2009) pp.347–40.

Reviews in *Asian Affairs*
Book Reviews

Islamic Fundamentalism. ed. R. M. Burrell. (Royal Asiatic Society 1989) and *Mystical Islam: An introduction to Sufism*, by Julian Baldick (I. B. Tauris, London 1989) Vol. 21 (1980) pp.187–193 [Review article].

The Trial of Benazir: An Insight into the Status of Women in Islam by Rafiq Zakaria (Sangam Books 1990) Vol. 22 no.2 (1991) pp.184–6.

Jinnah, Pakistan and Islamic Identity by Akbar S Ahmed (Routledge) Vol. 29 no.2 (1997) p.214.

Freya Stark A Biography by Molly Izzard (Hodder & Stoughton) Vol. 24 no.2 (1998) pp.222–223.

Favourite Wisdom by Deborah Cassidi (Continuum) Vol 35 no.2 (2004) pp.210–211.

To Begin the World Over Again: Lawrence of Arabia from Damascus to Baghdad by John C Hulsman (Palgrave Macmillan, New York 2009) Vol. 41 (2010) pp.465–468.

Exhibition Review

'Lawrence of Arabia: The Life, the Legend'. (a review of the exhibition at the Imperial War Museum, 14 October 2005 – 17 April 2006)'. Vol. 37 (2006) pp.72–75.

Lectures

As has already been mentioned [see p.83] Hugh lectured to many different societies, one of which was the '63' Club, a small paper-reading society, which ran from 1923–2000. It met on a Sunday evening once a month through the winter. Introduced to the Club by Adrian Steger, Hugh gave three papers, which were later printed privately:

'T. E. Lawrence: Some Centenary Reflections' (11 Dec 1988) (subsequently also delivered at Cambridge and Oxford).

'From Rome to Ringling and Beyond: A World History of the Circus' (13 Feb 1994) (dedicated to the memory of Count Andre Maximillian Larzard).

'There's Wind on the Heath, Brother: Vagabonding with George Borrow. The itinerant life, writing and times of the celebrated 19th-century author' (12 Jan 1997; dedicated to all vagabonds).

Other Publications and Newspapers

'Edwina's Sixtieth Birthday' *The Humber Register*, (Nov-Dec 1987 vol. XLVII, no.5, p.8) A further letter appeared in the *Register* in June 2012 (vol.73, no.3, p.7)

'To the Edge of Wakhan and Back' (22 July–12 August 1997) [off-print of report on The Royal Russell School CCF Expedition across the Hindu Kush]

'A Self-conscious Masterpiece' (4 April 1998) *Daily Telegraph*. [article on text of *The Seven Pillars of Wisdom*]

'Riding to the Founts of the Rivers of Paradise' (May 2002 p.22–24) *Pennant*, Journal of Forces Pension Society. [article about the Oxus and Jaxartes rivers]

Trade Secrets. From the Households of Choumert Square (2002) [a miscellany of tips by the residents. Six entries by Hugh Leach]

The Ultimate Traveller. Sir Wilfred Thesiger Tribute (October 2003) [printed tributes by members of the Travellers Club]

Henry St John Basil Armitage CBE. Obituary. SAF *Journal* (2005) p.33.

'Lawrence in Arabia' (October 2005) *History Today*

Dr Victor C Funnell's *New from the Pews* (2009): Special Supplement dedicated to two of Hugh's Remembrance Day sermons: 'Christianity in Iraq' and 'The Current Plight of Christians and other non-Muslim minorities in Iraq'

'Memoires of a Desert Intelligence Officer 1959–61' SAF *Journal* (March 2005 p.53)

'A Piquant tale of a Princeton Tourer' *Flutenews* (December 2006) edition 367/368. [article about Hugh's 1927 Vauxhall Princeton Tourer]

46 Strange and Amazing Facts from the 46 little cottages of Choumert Square (November 2007) Choumert Square Archives. Four entries by Hugh Leach.

The MECAS Memoirs 1944 – 2009

Hugh attended the Middle East Centre for Arab Studies (MECAS) in 1958–9 and 1961–2. In 2000, the MECAS Association published *Envoys to the Arab World, The MECAS Memoirs Volume II, 1944–2009*. Naturally, the Arabic language was a stimulus for his wider engagement with the Arab and the Muslim world. When MECAS graduates were invited to provide memories from their careers after MECAS for this volume, Hugh provided the following four contributions:

'The Hejaz Railway'. Saudi Arabia. pp.53–54.

'The Surviving Jewish Villages of the Yemen'. pp.68–74.

'Desert Intelligence Officer, Nizwa 1959–1961' Oman. pp.182–186.

'My Circus Britannia in Cairo' Egypt. pp.244–246.

Remembrance Day Sermons

At the turn of the year 1999/2000, Hugh gave a presentation 'Dionysius and Gregory: the Whens, Whys and Wherefores of Christmas and the Millennium'. This was followed in 2004 by 'Trumpeter, what are you sounding now?' which he delivered at his parish church in Hinton St George. In following years on Remembrance Sunday, from 2005–2011, the themes for his sermons were:

'Christianity in Iraq from the first century to today' (2005)

'War Poetry' (2006)

'The Current Plight of Christians and other Non-Muslim Minorities in Iraq' (2007)

'God and the Gun: The Role of the Padre in War' (2008)

'Reflecting on 70 Years since the outbreak of WWII and current issues in Iraq and Afghanistan' (2009)

'The Importance for Western Christianity of the Battle of Milvian Bridge, 28th October 312' (2010)

'How Religious Texts Can Be Conveniently Misinterpreted' (2011) (see Appendix D)

Letters to Editors

As well as maintaining a wide correspondence with his many friends, Hugh wrote frequently to national newspapers and magazines. The letters covered many topics; the following are known to have been published: 'Well Shod' (*The Times*, 21 Oct 1983); 'Better Armed' (*The Times*, 6 Jul 1993); 'Easy Going' (*Radio Times*, 6 Aug 1993; 'Islam and Birth control' (*The Times*, 8 Sep 1994); 'Sixth Sense' (*Daily Telegraph*, 22 Apr 1998); 'Najaf and Karbala' (*The Times*, 29 Mar 2003); 'Iraqis and Palestinians confirm appetite for democracy' (*The Times*, 4 Feb 2005) and 'MPs' (*Sunday Telegraph*, 7 May 2009).

'…it was the excitement of the house door clicking
shut behind him and the knowledge that he was free
to roam that meant everything to Hugh…'

Stephan Roman

INDEX

Figures in **bold** indicate illustrations and photographs